poems for adults of all ages

ian hindmarch

Cover design by Pete Michels

Printed in Great Britain by Biddles Books Limited,
King's Lynn, Norfolk

The Pomegranate

An ode from the Aussie poetaster Sidney Bridge, as told to Ian Hindmarch.

Even with the richest lexicon of cultured Strine[1]
folks say pomegranate will never come in rhyme,
unlike wine, crime, thyme and fine,
but, fair dinkum[2] possums[3], here is mine.
I've searched like a faithful literary hound
and an apposite rhyme I think I've found.
I'm well stoked[5] and tell you bloody oath[6].

A week ago I felt in need of rest and relaxation, so
I lobbed[7] a barbie[8] by a billabong[9] in the bush[10].
The sheilas[11] wore only knickers[12] and I looked perve[13]
dressed in budgie smugglers[14] and hoping for naughty[15].
I skulled[16] coldies[17] from an esky[18],
ate a chook[19] leg and smoked some mull[20]
and saw green kangaroos while I tripped.
Even the bruces[21] seemed willing and beaut[22].
Bities[23] in the sand made me glad I wore thongs[24].
I suffered sharp gyps[25] in my guts, not funny,
so I ran for the tin shed housing the dunny[26].
The chook was uncooked, or real bodgie[27] bad;
I felt really crook[28] and the urge to chunder[29]
swelled up inside like a head of thunder.
As I gazed into that galvanised zinc pail
my life flashed past, as if blown by a winter's gale.
I dare not move, I was immobile, as if carved in granite,
but I remembered my first time eating a pomegranate,
it was in England, with my angel-love[30], a pommy[31] Janet.

GLOSSARY

[1]*Australian English*, [2]*undoubtedly*, [3]*darlings*, [4]*mates*, [5]*very happy*, [6]*the truth*, [7]*visited*, [8]*barbecue*, [9]*stagnant pool*, [10]*uninhabited land*, [11]*girls or women*, [12]*underwear*, [13]*perverted*, [14]*tight-fitting swim trunks*, [15]*sex*, [16]*drank a beer down in one*, [17]*cold beer in frosted cans*, [18]*portable cold box*, [19]*chicken*, [20]*cannabis*, [21]*men*, [22]*gorgeous*, [23]*biting insects*, [24]*flip-flops*, [25]*pains*, [26]*outside privy*, [27]*poor quality*, [28]*ill*, [29]*vomit*, [30]*girlfriend*, [31]*a British person*.

Reflections on an Ancient Epitaph

Here, on his back, doth lay Sir Andrew Keeling
and, at his feet, his mournful Lady, kneeling.
But, when he was alive and had his feeling,
she laid upon her back, and he was kneeling.

(A tavern song round. Jonathon Battishill, 1738-1801).

Remember the pleasures and joys of unfettered lust,
not that all we become is just a speck of dust.
Remember, though our days are fleeting as meadow grass,
what in those green fields we entranced lovers caused to pass.

Remember the breathless trysts 'neath the gibbous moon,
when young love's nascent needs and urgent passions bloom.
Remember those whom it was better to have loved and lost,
especially ones memorialised in photos or notched bedpost.

Remember how you met *her* and seized that fateful day
and forgot about the morrow; the Fates always have their way.
Remember waiting for the postman's pregnant footfall
and your lonely vigil beside the phone out there in the hall.

Remember how desires meant restful sleep was all in vain
and in dark of night, you lobbed pebbles at her windowpane.
Remember the blank gaze while an earnest suit you'd press
and the joy when she acceded and whispered a firm 'yes'.

Remember all the poems and ink-smudged billets-doux
as you struggled with the sentience of 'How much I love you'.
Remember, though Time blows the vestiges of life away,
to celebrate living: let bliss and joy rule the passing day.

Remember no man is an island, if true love's embrace he felt,
he'll not forget those with whom in passion's heat he knelt.

Betrayals

The hollow wooden horse designed by sly Achaean deceit
was in the Trojan war seen as a ruse de guerre quite neat.
But, in hallowed halls where warriors praise Honour loud
'Beware of Greeks bearing gifts' is the sentiment avowed.

Samson for voluptuous Delilah's embrace did pine and lust.
She cared not: for Philistine coin she'd break his trust
and inveigle the secret of his fearsome biblical might
which vanished as a barber shaved his locks that very night.

The Nazarene was praying in Gethsemane, quite out of sight,
until revealed by Judas Iscariot with kiss like serpent's bite.
It was an unwarranted act of treacherous disloyalty,
funded by the temple priests' gift of a silver royalty.

Chivalrous knights on the First Crusade
had ingenious devices from sharp-edged metal made.
These they fitted to their spouses as belts of chastity
to save their loved ones from unsolicited debauchery
and reinforce, in their absence, the vows of marital fidelity
unless a perfidious locksmith was cajoled to set them free.

The bejewelled-fingered abbot of the ancient abbey
sported poxed nose, lecherous eyes, glutton's paunch quite flabby.
The wooden crucifix about his neck was but a symbolic token
of holy vows taken and, by his hypocrisy, long since broken.

Duplicity and irony stalk the realm of anarchy and treason.
At the intended premiere of the Parliamentary firework season,
G. Fawkes was exposed by a fellow traitor in the 'Gunpowder Plot'.
Guy is ever remembered, his explosive intentions some folk liked a lot,
but the name of Francis Tresham is now by and large forgot.

Betraying friendship's covenant is the most heinous of darkest sin.
'Brutus, is it really you who are next to push your dagger in?'

The Madding Mind

'Oh, young Lochinvar is come out of the West,
in all the wide borders his steed was the best'.
This poetic fragment hurtled from my subconscious.
to awareness by process quite autonomous.

My schoolboy self, now the focus of my inner eye,
felt a scalding-hot radiator against his thigh
as he gazed through an open classroom window
on memory of priory ruins preserved in amber limbo.

He writes on broad lined paper with leaky fountain pen,
about the fabled, sweating crews of brave Achaean men
from Ithaca, rowing the wine-dark sea in old black ships
hearing false-sweet Siren songs and spells from Circe's lips.

'Respond to the heart's dictates', says father to me, his son;
I do, and find my career as a knight's move sybarite has begun.
I dwell in pleasure domes to hear tales from Araby, far away,
where wide-eyed houri beckon in their own seductive way.

Flights of fancy are at their peak when burning midnight oil,
as a tired conscience allows temptation's serpent to uncoil.
'Reflect Mr Bunthorne', these are memories that will never fade,
their triggers lie hidden in subconscious' deepest shade.

Awareness flickers as mighty 'must' and inevitable 'shall'
wrestle Lady Blanche to keep my abstract mind in thrall.
Sweet Buttercup knows things are never as they seem.
My inner self is a whirligig of images seen as through a dream.

Knowledge, life's organiser, gained at Athene's shrine,
was much enriched by Bacchus' generous gift of wine
enabling participation in the jabberwocky's frabjous day,
and gossamer weaving and watching unicorns at play.

A moment, a mere winking of an eye, is all that's needed
to transform grey reality into a psychedelia, well seeded
with emotions, sentiment, myths, leaves from history's tree
and thoughts of Sister Phoebe; who the deuce may she be?

Fallow fields become canvases of meadow flowers
which are gathered by swains to line nooks and bowers
wherein they, with buxom maids, can hours in dalliance pass
no shame of green sleeves from kneeling, elbows in the grass.

Phantoms eddy in tableaux of scenes from Christmas last,
yellowing pictures show faint heart's losers from the past.
An 'In Memoriam' for lovers who were once loved but lost,
'Arrrr, Jim lad, don't dwell on the pain old loves do cost.'

Daydreams are pleasure's handmaids and sooth my brain.
Wool-gathering augments nostalgia and reduces mental strain.
Fancies also serve to assuage the daily harbingers of decay
as cold, bleak reality gnaws at the once sun-twinkling day.

An old alarm-clock heralds morning coffee and a slice of toast.
I am not alone, but joined with an ever-changing host
of Wits, Greek Gods, gourmands, Chaucer's pilgrim cast,
poets, divas and ghosts. Only Minerva's owl is steadfast.

As my imagined companions people my everyday world, I find
I am an island entire of myself: no Doctor D. that's not unkind.
My flights of fancy soar as dawn's fingers bring daylight
and persist 'till Hecate's spirits rule the dreams of night.

'Fair moon to thee I sing', silver Queen of the heavens
whose moonlight turns reason to sixes and sevens
and overloads my conscious brain to the point of overflow.
I lose my mind in visionary reverie that's only mine to know.

The Travelling Thespian

In darkling shadows
backstage at the Hippodrome
a fat knight waddles to and fro,
mouthing his lines as an aide memoire.
Playing a famous role is an acquired taste.

Under full stage floodlights
beads of sweat form on Sir John's brow -
larded with Leichner greasepaint foundation -
and coalesce in the warm privacy of his crotch.
Wearing a pre-worn padded suit is an acquired taste.

Aromas of erstwhile Falstaffs rise from kapok stuffing
as denizens of the *Boar's Head* tavern play their parts.
His voice is bitter - bile from a 'Horse's Neck' hangover
and curdled tinned milk from his acrid breakfast tea.
Acting in rep is an acquired taste.

The acned pimpleton playing Hal
delivers with Olivierian gusto the cutting line,
'I know thee not, old man',
to applause from the school party in row three.
Matinee performances are an acquired taste.

After final curtains, and the hair of several biting dogs,
the thespian retires to the warm embrace
awaiting in his well-bosomed landlady's bed.
He performs perfunctorily, at a measured pace;
his paramour's ample virtues are an acquired taste.

His landlady also makes a few bob doing his laundry
and sewing-on buttons that have become detached
from his threadbare Jermyn Street poplin shirts,
bought near the Haymarket just after the war.
Being down at heel is an acquired taste.

Landlady's daughter earns her spends on her back
providing a service for select old-gentlemen lodgers.
Her 'beau' runs betting slips for a crooked bookie
and wields a cutthroat razor when collecting debts.
Neither is an acquired taste.

It is grim in West Hartlepool when the fog settles in.
Once locals hanged a monkey, thought it a French spy.
They also 'hang out to dry' actors who 'die' on stage.
Northeastern audiences are an acquired taste.

The 'End of the Pier Show' in Weston-super-Mare
was Shakespearean highlights cum dancing girls' affair.
It started at ten thirty, with Macbeth's Folies Bergère.
A gas fire under the witches' cauldron set the pier alight.
Exeunt in flames was never to be an acquired taste.

A Modern Nursery Rhyme

Jack Spratt ate Mars bars deep-fried in fat,
his wife scoffed strawberries and cream.
An excavator dug a triple grave for the pair of them,
somewhere in Kensal Green.

haiku

shallow water pond
sky's crystalline reflection
frogs swim between clouds

moths flit aimlessly
grave-dark silence overwhelms
awaiting your call

koi carp in blue bowl
full crimson lips chalk-white face
brocade kimono

urban foxes bark
belfry bats dart sightlessly
doves roost in silence

flat-bellied lizard
bright green against brown sandstone
orange noonday heat

a dog's shadow falls
ever changing sunlit grass
unbounded movement

cows graze in meadow
new lambs skip on spindle legs
spring showers wash all

sun-dappled brown trout
floating caddisfly larvae
kingfisher feathers

hay wain in farmyard
chickens staccato clucking
sepia photos

marshland reeds rustle
bitterns boom in counterpoint
toads croak melody

white-furred winter fox
hidden in the windswept snow
but the hunters see

raindrops on fishpond
orange-gold carp blow bubbles
dark thunderclouds burst

barrel of monkeys
play in treetop canopy
forest leopards watch

lace-winged dragonfly
wide-mouthed tree frog anticipates
lily pad dining

koi carp in fishbowl
black orange-red white palette
sunset on a lake

croaking harmony
choir of frogs on bulrushes
serenade the moon

The Minotaur

Daedalus, designer of labyrinths supreme,
did construct at Cretan King Minos' behest
a prison maze, that some thought was his best,
to enclose and hold for ever more
Queen Pasiphaë's beast-child: the Minotaur.

This lustful royal wife had craved animal passion
and had herself inside a frame of cow's skin disguised
so to entrap Poseidon's white bull's thrusting thighs.
Of this illicit union the Minotaur, by the will of Gods, was bred:
a human torso and limbs, but a bull's tail and horned head.

The Beast was timid, shy and wary, even of the shadows cast
by tallow torches onto the walls of his granite prison vast.
Minos' daughter, Ariadne, by Cupid's dart was bewitched,
in her Beast's arms she imagined her humdrum life enriched.

She'd seen sacrifices sent to her love for his gourmet delight
and vowed this would change when she became his wife.
The Beast ate no greens so suffered stomach-ache each night,
was depressed with mental anguish and a poor quality of life.

As princess and cannibal, life experiences were limited,
but they eloped one spring evening, before it was dark,
to invest all their savings in a labyrinth-themed park.
Beast's human, protein-rich diet suited 'brain' as well as 'brawn'
and countless ideas for products his creative mind did spawn.

They marketed t-shirts, animal masks, Bull's Blood lemonade.
Their 'Horn and Hoof' bistro was a popular family venue
for Cretan cuisine: human sacrifices were not on the menu.
They'd often celebrate good fortune with a sumptuous feast,
thanks to royalties from Disney's *Beauty and the Beast*.

A Schoolboy's Memories of War

Aunt Mary lived with us and from spare cloth made the quilt,
that snuggled me close as I dreamt each night in bed.
I never knew Uncle Jim. He'd gone missing, presumed dead.
His black-edged photo gazed at me from frame of shell-case gilt.

Sometimes her patchwork coverlet became my nocturnal tent
when draped from brass bedframe and hoisted over my head.
There *George V's Jubilee Book* by flashlight beam was read,
vivid images of The Great War to sepia memory were sent.

A whiff of cologne and smell of *Erasmic* shaving cream
permeated the house following Dad's morning shave.
He used a cutthroat razor, which seemed so very brave.
He'd learned to wield the blade in Flanders' dawn's pink gleam.

Weather forecast on the wireless meant time for school had come.
I skipped past the Parish Church graveyard, with its ancient yew,
and the War Memorial: a cast bronze, life-size, soldier statue
representing someone's dead husband, father, lover, son.

Our teacher was a spinster. Dad said she was once 'quite a lass'.
Her fiancé sailed off to World War Two but never did sail back.
She taught everyone else's kids in a dress, chalk-dusted, black
and sometimes gazed wistfully in schoolroom window glass.

The Head taught science by experiments with smoke and smell.
He'd fought in the Great War and returned victorious and intact,
but though he had his body whole, his mind was sorely cracked;
he jumped at sudden noise and lived in an anxious, fretful Hell.

The Grammar School Hall was with Honours Boards full lined.
Lists of War Dead inscribed on polished planks of old elm tree.
'It is sweet and proper to die for one's country'.
A sentiment that took root in that erstwhile schoolboy's mind.

Return to Samarkand

A caravan lopes down sand dune tracks.
Desert shadows shimmer in rippling heat.
Bull camels with tinkling silver harness bells
carry tasselled, black-robed nomads on their backs.

Billowing silks and broidered gauzes
enshroud the hennaed purdahnashin,
whose smouldering kohl-lined eyes
tempt beyond the yashmak's rim.

The watchman in the Eastern tower
blows a brazen trumpet shrill.
Cedarwood gates thrown open wide
let the caravanserai amble in.

Merchants hurry for chests of money
to buy scented sweetmeats, boys, spices,
bales of silk, hookahs, blocks of hashish,
porcelain, pepper, poppy paste and pearls.

The setting sun gilds mausoleum mosaics
and casts shards of mote-filled golden light.
A muezzin, from the mosque's high minaret,
cries a melodious summons to evening prayer.

Camels snort, spit, bellow at their tethers
ranged round the empty market square.
Blue-indigo darkness falls cold and fast,
charcoals in pierced brass stoves burn bright.

On madrasah benches, pupils chant their last refrains.
Bleating lambs fall silent, as stew aromas skyward waft.
Assassins initiate a novice to the secrets of their craft.
By light of oil-dip Omar, the scholar, writes quatrains.

In the tanners' quarter, midst stench of urine pits,
charas smokers dream of a different daily lot.
Oud players strum sentimental tunes from times past
and sing wistful songs of love in dialects half forgot.

The old city stills, and a velvet silence covers all.
Moonlight turns landscapes silvery monochrome,
as janissaries in barracks sleep with measured breath,
rehearsing for that final duty call with timeless death.

Warm zephyrs from the western lands
bring perfumes of camphor and frankincense.
Houris dance to echoes of a zither's jangling strings,
their toes caressed by eddying sands of Samarkand.

A Victorian Intimation

A small envelope bearing a broad black edge,
an address inked out in finest copperplate
did a fearful anticipation from the mind dredge,
as to which kith or kin had now the epithet of 'late'.

Inside, a name on card engraved with churchyard yew,
a toppled urn, a coffin and shattered Doric column.
A skull and crossed bones show what Time's gifts all accrue.
An intimation of death is ritual notification quite solemn.

Crepe manufacturers and undertakers sport profit-puffed faces,
since Great Victoria set a fashion for funerals black and grand.
Snotty-nosed mutes watch horses set to a hearse's traces,
pallbearers in cloaks wear beaver hats with black silk bands.

The widow scatters dried flowers on her rosewood dining table,
and holds a fresh-cut-rose in her soft kid-leather funeral glove.
Such floral symbols of life and death keep quivering lips stable,
but hollow, moist eyes show the grief of loss of lifelong love.

Play With Moonbeams on the Bed – a Pantoum

Play with moonbeams on the bed
Pale skin blued by night's own light
Hearts rule all, by passion fed
Willing bodies, ne'er a fight

Pale skin blued by night's own light
Joined as one, by gesture led
Willing bodies, ne'er a fight
Fingers clutching, cheeks flushed red

Joined as one, by gesture led
Torrid feelings reach a height
Fingers clutching, cheeks flushed red
Pulses race in sheer delight

Torrid feelings reach a height
Dreams and yearnings fill the head
Pulses race in sheer delight
Of common sense the mind is bled

Dreams and yearnings fill the head
Desires rise like free-flown kite
Of common sense the mind is bled
Breathing quickens, eyes shine bright

Desires rise like free-flown kite
With urgent force three words are said
Breathing quickens, eyes shine bright
We're together till we're dead

With urgent force three words are said
Hearts rule all, by passion fed
We're together till we're dead
Play with moonbeams on the bed

The Windmills of Mykonos

Three thatched, white-walled windmills,
backlit by a bright Grecian sun,
threw brown, Maltese Cross, silhouettes
across our bedroom wall in the taverna
where, for the first time, we forged our love.

The wind sails, moved by a hilltop breeze,
made silent-movie patterns flash
on naked, bed-strewn bodies of
silent, stone-still, future dreamers.

My love, so mesmerised by your affirming smile,
remained lucid-true in the next day's light
and during the days and nights of the next fifty years.

We still lie together on Mykonos,
where hilltop windmills cast flickering shadows

to dance on our white stone grave.

Bacchus

Deep in the darkest forest glade,
where hairy centaurs rutt and roam,
there, where ancient myths were made,
young Bacchus lounged on bowered throne.

A godlike head fringed with golden braids
festooned in vines with a plaited-ivy crown.
His sylph-like limbs, proportioned like a maid's,
his beard, the merest wisp of ripe peach down.

He played Pan pipes as timorous dryads swirled.
Midst fallen pinecones he wrestled young blond men
and danced as cymbals clashed and bagpipes skirled.
The embrace of cross-dressing satyrs always in his ken.

Bacchus, doyen of vintners, cultivator of vine and grape,
zealously promoted wine for merriment and devilry.
Mankind, gifted the first cup, was left mouth agape,
singing paeans to their new-crowned God of Revelry.

An adoring army of bacchants, nubile female beauties,
became his retinue tending to all his worldly needs,
energetically performing the most intimate of duties
clad only in smiles and necklaces of pearled sweat-beads.

The appreciation of wine is the most jubilant of pastimes.
It looses tied tongues, grants courage to the faint of heart,
inspires poets to heights of Parnassus with artful rhymes
and lubricates erotic desire in the shy lover's private part.

With open arms, wise imbibers embrace wine in moderation,
evading sleep-promoting Hypnos and the brain's disequilibrium.
The music of life experiences sounds bright without gross intoxication
as, thanks to Bacchus, our wine-caressed minds wander in Elysium.

haiku

summer garden bees
birdsong insect heavy air
silent oil painting

a cordial sun
relieves cold grey tree-bound mists
forest life awakes

postcard-perfect sky
red roofs toasting in noon sun
wishing you were here

golden red sunset
crumpled copper ocean swell
parted coral lips

brown leaves drift earthwards
a final dance in sunlight
winter storms begin

crystal icicles
melting droplets in sunlight
rainbow-coloured tears

frozen shallow pond
turns gold in setting sun
nature's alchemy

sundial shadow
keeps fine track of hour of day
timeless dreams by night

pale rain-drizzled face
turned aside towards weak sun
salt tears washed away

seven stepping stones
lake island temple ruins
glow in setting sun

pale winter sunshine
horse-drawn plough makes deep furrows
rich brown Wessex earth

sunshine through shutters
sharp-edged bands of liquid gold
cross your peach-soft flesh

pale grey mist forms wraiths
pallid ghosts from childhood dreams
vanish in warm sun

sun-warmed sharp white sand
velvet abrasive soothes feet
tickling painted toes

embers of sunlight
broadleaf trees at eventide
your soft salt tears flow

Faustus - A Villanelle

Faust coveted a life immortal.
Elixirs and philtres he did sip.
He planned to escape death eternal.

Nostrums were noted in his journal
by gutt'ring flame of sheep-tallow dip.
Faust coveted a life immortal.

He conjured imps with spells cast verbal.
Round mystic pentacles he would trip.
He planned to escape death eternal.

He'd greet demons with kiss fraternal.
He must avoid The Fates' final snip.
Faust coveted a life immortal.

In black mass and coven nocturnal
with naked witches he'd swive and skip.
He planned to escape death eternal.

He signed in blood his soul's dispersal
to dark Mephisto's demonic grip.
Faust coveted a life immortal.
He planned to escape death eternal.

A Modern Nursery Rhyme

Jack said Jill should take the pill
so he could do things he shouldn't ought to.
She refused, but they still went at it with a will
and now they've a baby daughter.

Allusions For a Rainbow

Confused by noise from crowds cheering all round
a glossy black, sharp-horned bull paws the ground.
He's been made raging mad by stabbing and lancing
and mesmerised by toreadors' horses artful prancing.
With raw, instinctive aggression he charges and fights
the man in his sights dressed in shimmering suit-of-lights.
The fluttering cape hides, in the hand, a sharp-edged sword.
Death in the afternoon: the matador on the sand lies gored.

The Battle of the Boyne in Sixteen Ninety
belongs to King William and God Almighty.
Every twelfth of July, Ulster's proudest sons
celebrate, with marching bands, as the bowler-hatted ones
tramp down the Belfast streets with pride
and loud applause from those on the same-footed side.

He had deserted: from the Hun had run,
causing the death of his sergeant and chum.
They tied him tight to an old bentwood chair.
His sad-eyed distant gaze was fixed elsewhere.
Twelve mess mates, with rifles quite high-powered,
shot to death their erstwhile pal and coward.

Mad Carew stole the unripe eye of the idol god.
Naïve owl and pussy cat left in a boat of pure peasecod.
I sing about ten bottles standing on a wall,
while round my hat a band of willow I let fall.
There is a wise man with a dollar and gardener's fingers
who, on a piece of grass in the village centre, lingers.
He seethes with envy and would like the sward to putt on.
Hood's gang hide, dressed in dyed wool from Lincoln,
and plant a glasshouse full of legumes to make salsa sauce
to delay the visit of the scythed rider on the corpse-hued horse.

Einstein's distant female cousin
had the most magnificent bosom.
She danced nude in Paris City,
which led to Albert's theory of relative titty.

The cotton serge de Nîmes was pale as clotted cream
until well infused with an ancient Asian dye.
This helped Levi Strauss tailor his first cowboy's jean
and James Dean gain a trademark he'd be recognised by.

A five-petalled flower in the hedgerow there does hide,
as shy and sweet smelling as any blushing spring bride.
Other people can behave like flowers too,
some shirk limelight like an introverted shadow,
not because of hollow idleness or motives shallow,
but because their affinities shrink from the nervous loud,
and they retire from the glare of the madding crowd,
so unlike me and you.

The Bigot

The bigot wrote the text
fuelled by anger and envy,
it signified nothing.

The opening speech by the bigot
was full of clenched fists and furious words,
it signified nothing.

The bigot gave sworn evidence
based on lies and malevolence,
it signified nothing.

The bigot cast a vote
with hatred in the heart,
it signified nothing.

On Facebook the bigot had
seventy thousand followers,
it signified nothing.

The bigot died with a closed mind
their obsequies at the crematorium
signified nothing.

Poetry Thrives ...

...where oared quinqueremes ply the wine-dark sea
and tall tales are told of an antique land.
...where, in the Khan's dome, all pleasure is free
and white-bearded kings lie asleep in golden Samarkand.
...in graveyards where dead men haunt the timorous dairymaid
and moonlit yew tree roots wrap about pale bones.

...beneath a Wych elm tree's dark, spreading shade
and as kine wind o'er the lea neath silhouettes of Druid stones.
...by flick'ring candlelight and evening star
and moonbeams shining on the raging deep.
...by putting out to sea to cross the bar
and finding final rest in boundless sleep.

...as Chanticleer dreams of what is to come
and struts and crows among his concubines.
... when Nicholas is branded on the bum
and a Pardoner quaffs liquor of vines.
...when a highwayman rides the purple moor
and Bess plaits red love knots in her black hair.

...where she walks in beauty full of allure
and her kiss tastes of cherries full and fair.
...as life is measured out with coffee spoon
and yellow fogs caress the windowpane.
...as brown leaves tumble free one autumn noon
and love comes like sunshine after springtime rain.

...when rank cowards betray you with a kiss
and when you always hurt the one you best love.
...you'll let a kiss confirm an endless bliss
and resemble then the amorous dove.
...where shining Popocatepetl gleams
and Tyger burns bright in forest of night.

...where lotus eaters live their poppied dreams
and a yellow albatross stirs to flight.
...when unknown you're laid alone i' the grave
and the poet tells, for evermore you there now dwell.
...as laurel and cypress crown your final cave
and a funereal muse weeps her last farewell.

Attributions

Stanza 1
Cargoes: John Masefield, 1878-1967.
Iliad/Odyssey: Homer, c. 8th century BCE.
Ozymandias: Percy B. Shelley, 1792-1822.
A Vision in a Dream: Samuel T. Coleridge, 1772-1834.
The Golden Road to Samarkand: James E. Flecker, 1884-1915.

Stanza 2
Haunted: Robert Graves, 1895-1985.
In Memoriam and *Crossing the Bar:* Alfred Lord Tennyson, 1809-1892.
Sabrina: Edward Caswall, 1814-1878.
Elegy Written in a Country Churchyard: Thomas Gray, 1716-1771.

Stanza 3
The Canterbury Tales: Geoffrey Chaucer, 1340-1400.
The Highwayman: Alfred Noyes, 1880-1958.

Stanza 4
She Walks in Beauty: Lord Byron, 1788-1824.
Cherry Ripe: Robert Herrick, 1591-1674.
The Love Song of J. Alfred Prufrock: Thomas S. Eliot, 1888-1965.
Afternoons: Philip Larkin, 1922-1985.
Venus and Adonis: William Shakespeare, 1564-1616.

Stanza 5
The Ballad of Reading Gaol: Oscar Wilde, 1854-1900.
Those who love us best: from a quote by Ella W. Wilcox, 1850-1919.
Endymion: John Keats, 1795-1821.
Iolanthe: William S. Gilbert, 1836-1911.
Romance: W J Turner, 1898-1946.
The Tyger: William Blake, 1757-18270.

Stanza 6
Lotos-eaters: Alfred Lord Tennyson, 1809-1892.
The Rime of the Ancient Mariner: Samuel T. Coleridge, 1772-1834.
Upon His Departure Hence: Robert Herrick, 1591-1674.
Ave Atque Vale: Algernon G. Swinburne, 1837-1909.

Musical Innuendos: Pipe Dreams of Passion

Romantic passions root in music's fertile ground
when urged by a pipe organ's arousing sound.
Preludes use four manuals, a light-fingered touch,
with best harmonies achieved by going Dutch.

Lovers need a chest full of wind to out blow
breathtaking demands of toccatas played slow.
Variations on a popular tune can last all night
with vigorous fugues intertwining parts just right.
An open diapason can make eyes shine bright
and sustain a consensual crescendo of delight.

The resonant rumble of a sixty-four-foot pipe
can make lovers' shake with bass passion ripe
and cause their trembling bodies to gyrate
when the organ's coupled in 'Swell' to 'Great'.

The vox humana is reduced to a monosyllabic, 'Yes!'
as a perfect pitch leads to a coalescent caress.
Love's tempo can change from vivace to largo,
while intensity surges between forte and piano.
Though syncopated rhythms rule the beat,
finding a mutual final cadence is no mean feat.

Overall, love is Classical, late Romantic, con brio,
with some voluntary solos or swing-based trio.
Pulling out all the stops makes the organ linger,
but impromptu improvisation with a frenzied finger
enables da capo returns of the main theme,
but that's pure imagination, a real pipe dream.

haiku

crumbling mountain pass
tumbled boulders block the path
sounds ceased long ago

filberts ferns heather
autumn mists brown roast-chestnuts
stoat's white ermine coat

stags rutting loudly
bellowing primordial needs
man only whimpers

red holly berries
fresh white snow squeaks underfoot
golden hearth-strewn sparks

there's a space between
silent darkness and bird song
a sailor's false dawn

a skin-deep snowfall
smooth coverlet for graveyard
mosses wait for spring

tree ferns and heather
medlars persimmons bonfires
autumn has arrived

mirror-glass-smooth lake
purple hills lie upside down
rowboat floats in clouds

velvet snow wraps land
white-iced two-tiered wedding cake
honeymoon cherries

fireflies at nightfall
tiny golden dancing lights
sparks in bonfire smoke

a crystal-blue sky
soft winds shepherd clouds away
only contrails stay

straight ploughed furrow lines
dark primordial pattern
skin-deep tribal scars

buckwheat standing proud
no bowed heads before the storm
black grain useless now

flower-strewn meadows
under a thunder-black sky
insects buzz and drone

cold limestone cavern
clear underground stream gurgles
ageless stalactites

secret woodland path
briars strewn in ferny edge
scratch my naked legs

mud-spattered grasses
stinking hemlock hedge parsley
grow beside clay path

lavender dawn skies
tantalise the artist's eye
water colour wash

ink-black starless sky
nature's clothing for the night
covers up our deeds

powder snowflakes fall
crystal moonlight shines night sky
loud ice-cold silence

fir cone falls in pond
soundless ripples spread outwards
floating rootless seeds

crystal icicles
melting droplets in sunlight
rainbow-coloured tears

snow-laden cypress
branches drooping in sorrow
memento mori

Jack Frost's winter chill
tinkling springtime limestone rill
summer's sun-warmed lips

autumn woods resound
woodman's axe dog fox's bark
mushrooms push through mould

sharp flake ice crystals
mark edges of old windows
stark winter's cold eyes

broken fenland reeds
silent until the wind blows
pan pipes for satyrs

Similes for the Horns of Infidelity

'... like a punk, all keys will fit her trunk.'

'Cuckold's Haven'. Broadside ballad, 1638, London.

Did I not show you how to discriminate
between my bed and that of other men?
Will you ever see the difference
between marriage and serial infidelity?
Your choice of brutish lovers hurts me,
their coarseness leaves a bad taste in my mouth,

...like droppings in a parrot's cage.

I watch alone, through tear-stained eyes,
in the High Street's early-morning mists.
You leave the hotel in your post-coital guilt,
draped about his well-suited arm,
a shameless, brazen hussy.
Your broken vows and promises stink,

...like a midden in the noonday sun.

Ashamed of betraying our marriage vows?
You slept with my old school friend.
Only sex, not love, you said.
Was that after the first or tenth time in bed?
I do neither hate nor love you.
You're no longer of consequence,

...like a pee in a municipal swimming-bath.

I found letters in a shoebox
protesting his unrequited adoration.
Why did you continue to correspond?
Those sixteen years of written intimacy
completely betrayed our marriage.
Nothing now worth holding on to,

...like the aftermath of a hot vindaloo.

You did not visit our marriage bed in winter
when the deep snows gripped the land
and hail-strewn gales blew from Arctic wastes.
Instead, you stayed in his stove-warmed bedroom
and enjoyed a threesome with him and his sister.
You remain a pain in my fundament,

...like ice on the seat of an outside privy.

A Modern Nursery Rhyme

Little Miss Muffet
met a man at a buffet
while sipping her chardonnay.
He substituted whisky
which made her quite frisky
and then had his evil way.

Never Relinquished

Ensconced on the clipped-wool rug,
warmed by the *'Zebra'* black-leaded range,
Felix, the tabby tomcat, stretches and purrs
contentedly as firelight reflects in his green eyes.
The aura of languid, carefree, total relaxation
is purely a deception, so the unwary pay no heed
to the sharp-clawed paws ready to defend
his unalienable right to his place on the hearth.

Love's Last Embrace

Hushed chatter of friends, sentiments well meant.
A sharp white, fluorescent tube flickers overhead.
Wafts of *Cuir de Russie*, your especial scent,
linger and flow about my stark hospital bed.

The regular rhythmic gasps of respirator-driven air
- a hollow reminder of life's breathless finality -
wheezes like steam-driven organ at the spring fair
where we launched our love in youth's venality.

Mortality lurks in the bags housing my body's dross
and in dogeared charts plotting my inexorable decline.
Life's ravages eroded my body, but my mind knows no loss
as I recall a life well lived with tints of roses, love and wine.

On top of your beige Dior twinset, you've a flimsy plastic apron:
a green, surpliced confessor to shrive me on this world beneath.
You catch my eye, smile and mouth a lover's amorous token
as my eyelids close on the image of love you now bequeath.

I sense your moist coral lips press against my brow
as your body arches across mine in a crinkling embrace.
A ritual farewell, breaking the final seal of our wedding vow:
forever together, till Death takes one to a state of grace.

The Cardigan

An angora cardigan
in a pale pink knit,
slightly oversized,
was your trademark.
The bright red fingernails
seemingly seeking daylight
as they peeped out of sleeves
which hid hand, wrist and bangles.
A baroque fragrance of *Coco* played
overture to your presence:
tinkling laughter, the main theme.
Your love for him will never last.
I see you still quiver from *our* passion,
though that was distant past.

Anatomy of Death

The heart, so long the source of pulsing beat,
in that final darkness, stops.
The brain, where compassioned thoughts did form,
lies quiet, inert, forever stilled.
The lungs, which voiced a lusty life,
expand with vital breath no more.
The love, that once life's passions filled,
wanders, lost in the eternal void.

haiku

vellum-pale moonbeams
shadows cast on table tombs
songs only dead hear

cream-coloured moonlight
turns strawberries onyx black
in the bowl we share

lambent stars night sky
diamond pendant velvet dress
sparkle in dark eyes

silent fir forests
hungry grey wolves howl at moon
troika bells tinkle

moon in crystal ball
future times and memories past
together in time

halo 'bout the moon
rings of smoke rise from log fire
gold band round finger

pale yellow moonlight
brown shadows from bare-branched elm
candlelight bathes altar

sliver of new moon
bright stars move across the sky
brown bats keep vigil

Souvenirs of Paris, 1960–2019

Stale garlic, ozone, scent the Metro,
Chez Jean's bottle of finest Bordeaux,
King Louis' old stables in Place d'Armes,
Josephine's Château Malmaison farm.

Texans chewing gum on le Pont Neuf,
pommes frites, moutarde grise and daube de boeuf,
Les Invalides, Napoleon's tomb,
Luxembourg gardens, chestnuts in bloom.

Coming-out in historic Marais,
Impressionists in Musée d'Orsay,
late-night café jazz on the left bank,
Le Marché aux Puces, buying French Francs.

Sainte-Maure goat's cheese ash-rolled round a straw,
Trocadero Park, Fountains Warsaw,
a morning coffee reading *Le Monde*,
Quiche Lorraine washed down with bière blonde.

Pissoir in Boulevard Arago.
Le Procope for sorbet farrago,
escargots, carpaccio of trout,
smoked charcuterie with sauerkraut.

Montparnasse, pastis, *Le P'tit Zinc,*
Milady Fourrures full of fine mink,
artists' easels ranged by Sacré-Coeur,
Square Boucicaut with fellow flâneurs.

Les deux Magots, homage Jean-Paul S,
L' Auberge Bressane for poulet de Bresse,
the iconic 'Kiss' in Musée Rodin,
Aux Lyonnais for best black boudin.

Châtelet echoing to sounds of bongo drums,
street sparrows pecking-up brioche crumbs,
driving round Étoile in a cold sweat,
petite marmite, *Sourire* for croquettes.

Arc de Triomphe, bright flame undying,
Cirque Phénix, trapeze artistes flying,
Longchamp and a day of horse-racing,
Champ de Mars with lovers embracing.

Menus without a price for madame,
foie gras en croute from Périgord farm,
huge relief finding a sanisette,
pommes vapeur with jambon and raclette.

Pleasure and friendship at a grande bouffe,
sensual tastes of turbot aux truffes,
Sainte-Clotilde for a requiem mass
mindful music of what comes to pass.

Mixing with students from the Sorbonne,
green macarons, black tea from Ceylon,
vielle prune, a *Moulin Rouge* can-can,
Maison de Nôtre's vanilla flan.

McDonald's food in Champs-Elysées,
merkins in *Crazy Horse* cabaret,
mute taxi drivers - never a word.
Le Bristol's room prices are absurd.

Père Lachaise tombs: Piaf, Wilde and Ney,
flag waving at Bastille Day display,
armchair sightseeing from Bateaux-Mouches,
Maxim's ambience and amuse-bouches.

Fur-clad hookers in Avenue Foch,
champagne in *Le Grand*, feeling so posh,
gilded excess of La Madeleine,
browsing bouquinistes nearby the Seine.

Modern art at Centre Pompidou,
a pink-bowed caniche called "Miss Frou-Frou",
all the beautiful Parisiennes,
morning walks in the Bois de Vincennes.

Green Linnet Bar for Guinness and pool,
Tuileries garden for springtime boules.
Incense and candles in *Hôtel Costes*,
Palais Royale draped in winter frosts.

Queues for Eiffel Tower's top storey,
clams in *Le Dome's* belle-époque glory,
gaping at the Venus de Milo,
La Défense flats like painted silos.

Jésus de Lyons in *Le Train Bleu*,
bone marrow on toast, chef's pot-au-feu,
aproned garçons serving café au lait,
Sainte-Chapelle windows sunlit in May.

Hachis Parmentier in *Buvette,*
a blind date arranged with a soubrette,
L'Olympia theatre for chansons,
Buddha Bar lounging with 'le bon ton'.

Grand opera, Palais Garnier,
crêpes suzette soaked in Grand Marnier,
the great organ sounds of Saint-Eustache,
La Barbière for a waxed moustache.

Folies Bergères, a glass of cognac,
Paul Bert Serpette's antique bric-à-brac,
a whole-pig feast, a real gourmand's meal,
everything eaten save piggy's squeal.

The frescoed dome of Le Panthéon,
round tins of sugared-violet bonbons,
'Pin-ups'and films of Brigitte Bardot,
beat poems sung by Juliette Gréco.

Shoppers with baguettes tucked under arms,
Rue Crémieux's pastel-coloured charms,
Bar Vendôme, right next door to the *Ritz,*
for black olives and Noilly Prat spritz.

Beluga caviar sold in grams,
burnt-stone skeleton of Notre-Dame.
Her last embrace, *Café de la Paix,*
knowing full well I would leave, not stay.

4/5/2019.

Love à la Française

I remember Spring in the apartment in Saint-Germain-des-Prés,
your artist mother told us tales of her Catalan satyr called Pablo.
Our love blossomed; youthful passions held us in their sway;
we abandoned inhibitions and let naïve emotions flow.

Nothing reflected candlelight better than your hazel eyes.

Your shimmering dressing gown, tailored from mulberry silk
and dyed a midnight, vitriol-black to match your raven hair,
wafted exotic fumes from a Sobranie, or something of that ilk.
Aromas of Chanel parfum eddied desire as you draped in a chair.

"Nothing is worn by those in love," you said, as you lay naked.

Smoky scent of latakia and yenidje leaf permeated your bower
while notes of jasmine and neroli impregnated your core.
You a muse-concubine, I a writer subjugate to your power.
We planned futures over coffee and croissants in Café de Flore.

"I'm sorry we must part now," you said, "there is another."

A 'no regrets' memory of heady floral aromas of fragrant incense
and my mind flits to a boudoir where an houri plied her art.
My new muse eschews sensual excesses and performance intense,
it is with love's plain passion that she enslaves mind and heart.

A Modern Nursery Rhyme

Hey, dub a dub dub,
three guys went for a rub
in a local Reiki bar.

They were massaged and oiled
and their stiff muscles uncoiled
but two thought the rubs went too far.

The third was so lavish with his spending
he was awarded a free happy ending,
which exceeded his life's expectations by far.

Boulder, Colorado

'Pamela-Ann, Pamela-Ann,
she gets stoned whenever she can.'
Conjured eternal truths which did them amaze
as their minds wandered in acid haze
among the clouds on Estes Park peak
'Wow', the only word they needed speak.

Shades of silver miners long time still
shrouded 'bout the tunnelled hill.
Remains of saloon, church, jail and old graveyard
stood as witness to lives once lived so short and hard.
In that derelict cabin, beset by windblown tumbleweeds,
they'd food, drink and 'orange tabs' to satiate their needs.

The cry of a timber-wolf, or a lost banshee's wail,
echoed in frost-edged night as they tripped beyond the pale.
The Congolese *Missa Luba* played on a small cassette player.
The Mass formed a rich brocade of psychedelia, layer upon layer.
Sex was no longer a dutiful, missionary undertaking
but a rhythmic *Benedictus* of understanding and creating.

A blood-warm vortex of tam-tam beats did their bodies hook.
Cleopatra's grip was instinctively displayed, not from any book.
Eiffel's Tower waxed and waned at whim of pulsed machine.
Freud's synaesthetic text urged their needs were as they dream.
Fairytale images from bubbling cauldrons did ooze and flare
as the maelstrom of the *Gloria* did their very beings ensnare.

Waking was sleeping, perceptions forever changed by the trip,
mundane reality returned, drip by monochrome drip.
The *Missa Luba's* insight about their minds still prowls
as *Credo* bursts forth in parliament of Minerva's wise old owls
to flood the mind with memories of kaleidoscopes of sounds
and of Nirvana, a cabin, where flower-strewn Love abounds.

A Summer's Night on Penhill

There is a warm stillness in the air
enfolding the crags of Yorkshire's Dales.
As a summer's humid daylight languid fails
the dog fox and his vixen creep from their lair.

Emergent moonbeams' silvered hues
highlight ancient lichened drystone walls
and turn huddled hillside Swaledale ewes
to indigo clouds of curl-horned, woolly balls.

Cracks in distant Heaven's pearly door
let twinkling celestial starlight through.
A tawny owl nestles owlets born quite new
downy snug on their nest-hollow's floor.

A sandstone farmhouse, rambling large,
built four-square 'gainst the winter's spates,
absorbs the noontime sun's supercharge
in stifling air under roof of best Welsh slates.

A full tester, patinated oak, feather bed
squats centre room, mattress ropes tied sleep-tight.
Its bowed boards show it has served its masters well,
an easeful stage for birth, death and wedding night.

I never sleep alone, though my bedfellow is inconstant,
sometimes playing hide-and-seek until dawn breaks.
For several nights, we've conjoined in each other's arms,
but now, on a whim, she sees fit to shun me in my bed.

Fine Egyptian cottons swiftly wick moisture from the air
and my blood-warm sweat creates a moist, adhesive sheet
which manoeuvres into skin crevices unknown to me by day
and abrades fleshy parts modesty keeps hidden out of sight.

How can I entice my fickle seductress to join me in a tryst,
Even though a night in her arms is but practice for the tomb?
Beguile me shy mistress Sleep, I'm an avowed nocturnal hedonist,
seeking but peaceful rest from your embrace in my bedroom.

The Descent of the Man, Dr Charles Darwin

Charles Robert Darwin, the *soi-disant* evolutionist,
waited at Heaven's portal while the angel scanned his list
of those souls God had judged pure and fit for life eternal.
Those not named, through trapdoor fell to realms infernal.

"It's a paradox to say," wise St Peter kindly said,
"life will seem much better now you are truly dead.
You're down for Paradise on a set tariff for evermore
but, in your especial case, there is something else in store.

"You once wrote that the six days taken by His Almighty Nibs,
in creating the Universe, was nothing but false news and fibs
and you claimed that mankind was descended from Great Apes
which, given His efforts in Eden, seems like a load of sour grapes.
Fortunately, God has an excellent sense of ironic humour
and you've landed in clover excused your naïve bloomer.

"You'll not be fitted with Gabriel's aerodynamic wing implants.
There's no harp-plucking, polishing halos nor cherubic chants -
You're now in charge of primate breeding in the Elysian Zoo;
take care of your forebears and procreate with them too.

"Conceiving primate offspring is not as easy as it seems,
though the Great Apes share almost all of mankind's genes
and their notions of love and fidelity are highly intellectual.
The problem is male silverback gorillas are wantonly bisexual."

The Druid's Choice

In woodland clearing by the old oak,
a lichen-rusted, grey stone circle stands.
This Druid's ring is shunned by simple folk
since blood's spilt there by priestly hands.

On Midwinter's Eve the wise ones come,
wind-wizened faces, gaits quite spry,
their presence told by beat of drum
and shrill ram's horn cry as they pass by.

In the spring of the year just past,
the golden sun had been turned to night
as a dark circle over its shining face was cast
and home, village and field were deprived of light.

One seer is mute, another's deaf, the third can't see,
they know nature acts out her own capricious whim
but, as they sit beneath the bare-branched, ancient tree,
they ponder if day turned to night was ominous omen grim.

Gods of Mother Earth, to whom all men bend the knee,
are invoked while runes are read and bones are cast.
Incantations and spells are voiced three times three,
as elixir of nightshade and mandrake root is mashed.

The seers drink deep and gain insight from their trances.
To appease the Gods and threat of night perpetual allay,
a sacrifice of a woad-blue virgin, who about the old oak dances,
will be made by fire to turn night's shadow into sun-filled day.

As with a single voice the mystic trio recite the ancient rhyme
'Hap and hazard choose a fair-faced maid, to fire's embrace to go
so trenchant night will yield to springtime's lustrous prime.
Our just hands, join as one, pick ... Eena, Meena, Mina, Mo.'

The select maid was given poppy milk and dressed in tunic white,
her hair was crowned in mistletoe and holly sprig, well berried.
Flames beneath her wicker cage burned red and gold and bright,
as to funeral halls of pagan gods her sacrificed soul they carried.

Ernst and Heidi: A Tale of Swiss Wurst

Bare-chested Ernst, dressed in lederhosen,
collected his favourite flower,
edelweiss, by the dozen,
to decorate sweet Heidi's bower.

Satisfied with his floral decoration,
Ernst dined on beer, cheese and a full-fat wurst,
his best-loved lunchtime cold collation.
He ate so much his lederhosen seams did burst.

Ernst dressed rawhide style, without a thong.
Now naked, he posed godlike with his alpenstock,
a rod-like weapon of a hand-span's girth and enviably long.
He'd spied his love, Heidi, a shepherdess, with her flock.

Her ewes were well served by a heavy-horned ram,
a bell on a rope was round its muscled neck low slung.
Ernst's seemingly aggressive display of masculine élan
caused the tup to charge; nude Ernst's funeral knell rung.

But Ernst stepped aside to avoid a ram's horn-dealt crunch,
and swung his mighty weapon to knock the beast cold out;
then, without further hesitation, he continued with his lunch.
Ernst hoped Heidi would realise what his display was all about.

Heidi had never been in analysis, nor seen such a primaeval sight,
the weaponry impressed; she chose to live as Ernst's spouse.
Heidi could not imagine a better pursuit, for a cold Alpine night,
than the game 'hunt-the-wurst' in the bedroom of their house.

haiku

crumpled red silk dress
disordered cotton bedsheets
tear-stained pillowcase

with no future tense
Japanese live here and now
boutique love-motels

sea-mist born phantoms
echo The Dutchman's trials
spectres of lost loves

Japanese woodcuts
erotic titillation
fragile rice paper

geisha bedroom book
bold Kunisada woodcuts
two-dimension sex

myrrh clove cinnamon
exotic eastern perfumes
lurk in your cologne

love against all odds
opposites of a great truth
together as one

her concupiscence
frustrated by the armour
of his hair-shirt faith

tears in your brown eyes
reflect bedside candlelight
and grey of false dawn

a sleep without dreams
a world without birds singing
a life without love

seaweed by the door
wet or dry with weather change
or your love for me

algebra well learned
poems scan so perfectly
kissing only fair

monosyllabic
dress kohl men hair sun wax lips
a single woman

garden bonfires burn
russet leaves turned to grey smoke
my tears not for you

painted lips pressed firm
a Cupid's badge of scarlet
on her lover's cheek

your clove-scented breath
and green silk harem trousers
make me a sultan

storms roar at midnight
ever I neglect your lust
impatient mistress

ears of golden wheat
deaf to the breeze's whispers
sighing of our love

Tanka*

Amber, yellow, brown
wind-dried, wrinkled, fallen down
cones and leaves heap on the grass.
Crackling bonfire sparks fly bright.
Parkin cake on Guy Fawkes Night.

Stormy wine-dark sea
black ships pitch on Priam's shore
brought by Helen's fate.
Achilles kills brave Hector,
Troy betrayed by hollow horse.

Blue willow-tree plate
island teahouse lies in lake.
Eloping lovers
flee from father wielding cane
across bridge to safety.

Royal soldiers march,
pipers skirl a sad lament,
muffled drums thud loud,
funeral cortège passes,
The Monarchy carries on.

*Tanka are classical Japanese short poems of
five lines with a 5/7/5/7/7 syllable count.

Spring Forward

an acrostic with names of Old English Apples

Sweet *Annie Elizabeth* adored the start of Spring.
Perhaps, as *Granny Smith* claimed, she was conceived under a
Red Pearmain by *Lord Derby,* or *James Grieve,* or *Arthur Turner.*
Isaac Newton would have marvelled at her ripe *Ribstone Pippins.*
Now, with *Irish Peach* complexion, she attracted suitors like bees
Gathering nectar from a *Bramley's Seedling.*

Fortune favoured this *Norfolk Beauty;* she found her *Prince Albert,*
Orchard fruit-juice maker, Dicken *Cox.* He'd a good firm body,
Russet skinned, sharp as a *Grenadier.* The pair grafted together.
Wed in *St. Edmund's* with Parson *Peasgood Nonsuch* officiating.
A reception at *Stirling Castle* had catering by *Keswick Codlin.*
Relaxing on honeymoon in *Blenheim,* the bride learned to love
Dicken's cider.

Love's Calculus

At night, love's ebbing tide
leaves bare the sands of truth
and as you lie naked by my side
you whisper 'bout the passions of your youth.

With wistful smiles and moist-rimmed eyes
you detail fornication vigorous and free.
The number of partners totalled gives surprise
and my mind turns rancid green with jealousy.

'Only sordid sex, not love that will for ever last,'
you murmur sweetly, 'now it's just you and me.'
I leave when I calculate scores from your past
show I'm lover number three hundred and three.

Time To Stop

He was lying on a rag-clip rug
before the sea-coal-fired range.
Lead soldiers ranked in formation snug,
fought battles with boyish tactics strange.
"Put your toys away now," Mother said,
"It's time to stop, get off to bed."

He read that somewhere in a fabled land
Sinbad found the rare Roc's egg
and saw a golden city midst shifting sand
with abundant treasures by the keg.
"Put your book away now," Mother said,
"It's time to stop, no more reading now in bed."

His sister had smiles sweet as apple pies
she thumbed her nose and made a dare,
feeling safe as the apple of her parents' eyes.
"He said beastly things and pulled my hair."
"Don't tease your sister," Father said,
"It's time to stop or you're straight to bed."

Her soft grey hair, fresh washed, thin
moved slightly in the open-window air.
The crisp linen sheet pulled close to her chin
framed the peaceful, closed-eye stare.
"I don't want tears," Mother had said,
"it's time to stop." She died in bed.

Sunbeams dappled his college quad.
He played cards at tables of green baize,
suited in sub-fusc with socks eccentric odd.
He'd squandered time on revision days.
Answer three questions the rubric had said,
It's time to stop, put your pens to bed.

They met at a dance at the Nurses' Home,
love at first sight was a fitting cliché.
They skilfully schemed to be together, alone,
and for intimacy both in earnest, did pray.
At last, with fond urgency, she lovingly said,
"It's not time to stop, let's go up to bed."

Famous Spanish Composers

There's much to admire in the work of the music smith
who goes by the name of Albéniz.
The vibrant flamenco rhythms of de Falla
are as aurally tasty as well-spiced paella.
It is easy to adore the passion and Iberian gloss
of the romantic *Spanish Dances* of Granados.
The echoing intensity of the vocal masses of Victoria,
lift listeners' souls to peaceful euphoria.
Tárrega's intimate works for classic guitar
attract young lovers from near and afar.
Rodrigo from an early age was blind
but his haunting harmonies stay forever in mind.
Sor wrote diverse baroque music scores galore,
his operas, songs and ballets remain fresh for evermore.
But, best of all, towering above the herd by far,
is the English maestro the Spanish call 'El Gar'.

haiku

Ur Babylon Rome
stimulate strong images
not so Sunderland

leafless avenue
lamp-post trees shelter no birds
by night vixen barks

springtime in Paris
rustle of tissue paper
candy-striped hat box

sense the solitude
hear birds see stars smell flowers
beware virus hides

ears of golden corn
eyes on King Edward main crop
nose of Bordeaux wine

anthems and incense
old oak-trussed hammer-beam roof
gothic harmonies

stars in desert sky
oiled leather camel harness
Arabian night

old damp plaster wall
a map of America
outline in black mould

green wood in fire pit
smokes out al fresco diners
and summer midges

dark stone-pine branches
silhouettes in setting sun
bright pink neon flash

in Panama hat
with blue wisps of cigar smoke
I dream in Spanish

hammer on anvil
remembered sounds ring in ear
blacksmith's village forge

pipe organ grumbles
amber incense perfumes rise
vaulted ice-cold nave

bowl of double cream
strawberries lie half-covered
awaiting sugar

anaemic flowers
roadside thistles straw-stalked grass
breathe car's exhaust gas

Japanese gardens
pebble islands gravel seas
dry white sand rivers

fifteen sea-washed stones
positioned in the mind's eye
patterns with meaning

Pandora

Dark Chaos ruled the cosmic void
before that first pink-fingered dawn
developed like some primordial Polaroid
to proclaim immortal beings were born.

Helios began his daily circuit of the skies
driving the wild-horsed chariot of the sun.
Life was sustained by natures fecund supplies.
Destiny for Gods and Men by The Fates was spun.

Only immortal men flourished down on earth.
A Golden Age, where hawk nested with dove.
Of divine goodwill there was no dearth
as Gods reciprocated men's respect and love.

Goddesses bathed freely in woodland streams
and embraced the scented Zephyr's whispered sigh.
A timeless life was lived by all as in primordial dreams,
but Fortune's favour was lost in a twinkling of an eye.

Zeus' lightning raged on Olympus' height
when Prometheus stole fire from the Gods
and gifted it to men, causing them much delight;
men were now free, no longer God-dependent clods.

Zeus felt his status had been diminished
and planned revenge with retribution's knife.
His omnipotence was dented, though not finished,
but men would now enjoy but a finite life.

From clay and fire Zeus fashioned a mortal woman.
Perfection: crowned with pearls, in silver gown,
rose-blushed cheeks, fair skin perfumed with persimmon,
fine spun golden hair soft to touch as thistledown.

She'd many God-given gifts and unparalleled beauty,
was playful, naïve and unaware of Zeus' vengeful intent
but knew how to turn heads by shaking her booty.
To destroy men's immortality, to earth she was sent.

Men, seized by wonder at all she possessed,
called the hand-forged woman Pandora, the 'all endowed'.
To Prometheus' brother she was by marriage blessed.
To Zeus, Pandora was his vengeful thundercloud.

Zeus had gifted her an old, sealed wine jar
which he decreed she must never open.
He knew Pandora would ignore the rule by far
and what for men the open jar would betoken.

Zeus' jar was full stuffed with all things evil:
hate, greed, strife, wrath, lust, jealousy and death.
Pandora released them all, her curiosity a devil's weevil,
and men were plagued by old age, pain, and rationed breath.

Great Zeus had his revenge, felt mighty once again
as mortal men learned that beauty is only skin deep
and the Gods' largesse can give both pleasure and pain,
though the gift of a woman is decidedly one forever to keep.

Learning the Truth About Love

Was our love from a time of unfettered free will,
or were we puppets in a labyrinth of futile hope?
We pledged our lives, which were never ours to give,
and said, "I do love you," as we imagined a quick elope.

Or was it nothing more than Cupid playing us false?

How can I weigh the essence of a broken dream
when my lovesick heart to my mind speaks treason?
Through my lover's eyes things are never as they seem;
falsehoods masquerade as truths, desires serve, not reason.

Nothing lies unforgotten in my archives of loves lost.

A Poetic Whimsy from Old Asturias

This poem from an incunabulum, published by Estas Bromeando in Oviedo in 1499, is unique. The original was written in Bable, the ancient language of Asturias. Furthermore, all line-endings in the translation rhyme with Asturias.

Don Jose, a married Spanish hidalgo, lived in Old Asturias.
He dressed in velvet and leather with a noble's steel cuirass.
Instead of fancy rapier he sported a weighty naval cutlass
and drank of local cider enough to float a mighty galiass.
His refined and precise diction was clearly upper-class.
The literary salon in his hacienda equalled Montparnasse.

He collected marble statues and portraits in oil paint on canvas,
da Vinci's 'smiling woman' hung in an alcove behind a silk arras
to hide her from avaricious clerics and the curious criminal class.
Hilda, his young, blonde-haired Alsatian wife, was a country lass
and alchemist who, at time of writing, had not found gold, alas.
Her dowry was family vineyards in the distant valleys of Alsace.

One Holy day the Don sat his jackass to town via a steep crevasse,
and past geese kept to warn against thieves likely to trespass.
In a rustic inn he breakfasted on Pata Negra, chorizos, tapas,
morcillas, a beefsteak from a wild corrida bull raised on grass,
artichokes, fresh boiled fava beans and patatas bravas.
On the morrow he'd feast on boiled heads of fresh sea bass.

Later, Don Jose, in church attending the Holy Saint's Day Mass,
was seated in his family pew crafted in bog-oak from a morass.
He heard a loud gastric gurgling, felt gas deep in his gut amass
and prayed hard to the Saint for relief, but no aid came to pass.
Noxious fumes, trapped betwixt oak and cheeks of his carcass,
erupted with explosive force, like crumhorns played en masse.

It disturbed the belfry bats and shattered the priest's wineglass,
and stank like tanners' tubs which did the Don embarrass
but in formulating excuses, he was an expert none could outclass.
"Count your blessings it wasn't my wife, all comers she'd surpass
in the intensity of smells which creep out of her ..."

The remaining printed text is illegible because of substantial worm damage to the broadside itself. An unknown, near-contemporary, hand had, fortunately, completed the translation of the final stanza with a couplet written on a fragment of vellum and pasted onto the original.
It reads:

"In the intensity of smells which creep out of her alembic of glass
when she kills plague rats with clouds of poison gas."

The Sleeps of Man

Dad's spitting image: first-born, heir and son,
in his mother's arms he slumbers all day.
His trunk then tagged for school so far away,
nights in dorm beds bring his asthma on.
He takes love's sleep when Cupid's work is done.
A soldier's prowess is a sweaty, nocturnal display
as he fights in nightmares in corpse-encrusted clay
where bayonets wield death under a blood-red sun.

A lawyer's wig is earned by dining-in,
his apnoeic snores make loud, nasal din.
He sleeps through lunch and dinner on a whim,
and on the bench, too, when colleagues bore him.
Death claims his dear friends: Time opaques his eyes.
He wakes anew each dawn, until the night he dies.

The First Bicycle Day*, 19.iv.1943

Albert Hofmann, Swiss Chemist and PhD,
was developing new drugs from ergot fungus.
With attempt twenty-five he discovered LSD
and a pathway to The Gods did open before us.

Just two hundred and fifty millionths of a gram
turned the Rhine into a pathway of watered gold silk.
His mind with kaleidoscopic images did cram
as he saw his lab through a mist of pinkest milk.

His distorted perceptions caused him concern.
Albert felt he'd joined the sensory silly season
with nothing to counter this schizophrenic turn
which challenged the integrity of his reason.

He needed sanctuary: his home too far to hike.
As a World War raged, cars were hard to find,
so Albert chose to ride his trusty, well-oiled bike
just as the drug's effects began to swamp his mind.

His bicycle was as if by breezes moved
though no wheels turned as streets passed by.
The April sun caused him to feel loved
and he saw the taste of Baseler Leckerli**.

There was a presence felt above and about him,
as if a daemon lurked from a Faustian night.
Lucidity was fitful, at the mercy of a chemical whim,
his consciousness expanded like an eager floodlight.

Feeling like Alice in her wonderland
He asked of a green caterpillar, who am I?
Time passed as slowly as grains of sand
leaching through a rusty needle's eye.

Hoffman's experiences on the two-hour bike-ride home
were not the effects of lysergic acid that his sponsor needed.
Albert recorded all in his journal, which became well-known
and calls to 'turn on and drop out' were universally heeded.

*Bicycle Day, 19 April. Name given to the Anniversary for the commemoration of the discovery of LSD.
**Baseler Leckerli is a traditional sweet biscuit filled with nuts and candied fruits.

The Earworm

I'd an earworm tune going round in my head
I'd been afflicted since yesterday morning.
My girlfriend had put on Mahler, while we were abed.
"It's Gustav's First," she'd chirped, "instead of sex.
I'm not really in the mood for fawning."
No, I thought, it could be the mood where you are 'ex'.

A double bass played the tune 'Frère Jaques' in the minor,
and the 'dormez-vous' worm was born, an aural itch.
Though the ancient tune could find no expression finer.
From a joyful children's nursery game prance-around
Mahler had conjured up a funereal dirge the senses to unhitch.
In my head Brother James' matins bells did involuntary resound.

Throughout the day the tune rang relentlessly in my mind;
my brain, by endless rounds of din-dan-don, was jaded.
Even with aid of claret bottle no aural respite could I find.
Exhausted, I'd no need to count any of Bo-Peep's sheep
As, in Sleep's warm embrace, the earworm finally faded.
In the morning my uncluttered mind could soar and leap.

That evening I took her to dinner in town, at the Ritz.
I'd felt guilty about thinking of ending our tryst.
Afterwards we went to the cinema for a film on 'The Blitz'.
On the way home she repeatedly sang, as a single-voiced choir,
'London's burning, London's burning, call the engine,
call the engine; fetch water, fetch water; Fire! Fire! ... Fire! Fire!'

She couldn't get the 'London's Burning' tune out of her mind,
it was a round, like the Brother James' Air I now did dread
and, without bidding, 'Frère Jacques' reprised again in my head.
It is said by the ancients, and I agree, that true love is really blind.
But love is not deaf and, though I might seem callous and unkind,
I've decided, without further delay, to change my partner in bed.

I Heard the Toll of My Funeral Knell

I heard the toll of my funeral knell.
A tenor peal ringing deep in my head.
I stood on gallows, the brink of hell.
Judged for my crime: to be hanged till dead.

A tenor peal ringing deep in my head.
To wake a secret, she'd now not tell.
Judged for my crime: to be hanged till dead.
I choked her when the belly did swell.

To wake a secret, she'd now not tell.
"I'm yours for ever," she oft times said.
I choked her when the belly did swell.
We loved with passion, to others wed.

"I'm yours for ever," she oft times said.
I stood on gallows, the brink of hell.
We loved with passion, to others wed.
I heard the toll of my funeral knell.

A Modern Nursery Rhyme

Mary had a lambswool coat wherein was a kilo of snow.
Everywhere that Mary went the coat was sure to go.
She took it down to school one day
where there was a market for drugs Class-A.

haiku

autumn-cold dark sea
wave crests blown ashore on rocks
spume-misted soft lips

royal-blue sea swell
scudding yacht's white wind-taut sails
submerged coral reef

unknown-blue ocean
colours change with rising sun
silent revision

moonlight bleached shingle
sea-washed pebbles purple white
storm cones hoisted high

storm-blown salty spume
scouring paint beachfront huts
sculpting shingle banks

footprints in the snow
tide lines marked in seashore sands
life verse on gravestones

soft midnight silence
loud roar of waves on lashed seashore
less is always more

grey lagoon water
black gondolas lurch sideways
beetles on millpond

A Mediaeval Litany

Charcoal-burner chops green alder wood,
children play games in riverside mud.

A cunning man harvests blue wolfsbane,
coppiced osiers yield basket cane.

An old witch ducked twice in cold mill pond,
liegemen pledge their Lord a fealty bond.

Mutton-fat dips light weavers night work,
lad touched by imps runs wild and berserk.

Falconer knots on jesses and bells,
common middens leach out gagging smells.

Chantry monks sing for the recent dead,
beggars dream of loaves of manchet bread.

Proud yeomen archers clutch six-foot bows,
levied soldiers armed with scythes and hoes.

Street urchins follow a hue-and-cry,
fine linen cloth bleached in wood-ash lye.

Serfs gather fresh rushes from the fen,
privies emptied by gong farmer's men.

Tomb-top effigies without a smile,
sore piles healed with salve of camomile.

A thief grasps knocker on minster door,
gains sanctuary by ancient law.

Cheating wife judged by hot-coals ordeal,
praying 'gainst hope her blisters will heal.

A tooth-puller plies his painful trade,
from piss-soaked hides soft glove-leather's made.

A cutpurse is caught, feathered and tarred,
bold destriers fret in castle yard.

Alchemist's foundry with furnace bright,
novice nuns hide in veils of pure white.

Sacred mysteries of the Latin mass,
Canterbury pilgrim rides a grey ass.

Fishmongers sell lampreys, tench and eels,
lovesick maidens dream at spinning wheels.

Priest's tithes amass him earthly treasures,
trulls, doxies and bawds trade poxed pleasures.

Noah survives flood in mystery plays,
troubadours swoon and sing love-lorn lays.

Peasants stamp out old round dance measure,
making the most of Saint's Day leisure.

Brides bedecked with ribbons and nosegays,
fools with pig's bladders voice donkey brays.

From the shambles come piglets' squeals,
everything else is used for folk's meals.

Curd-scented milkmaid flirts with young squire,
rosemary-strewn corpse lies in church quire.

Rabbit warrens spread on common land,
arcane rituals with hanged man's hand.

Starving poacher tickles Lord's brown trout,
birds in castle dovecote preen and pout.

King's Herald dressed in tabard of red,
bed bugs abound in the inn's common bed.

Wolfhounds gnaw beef bones under oak table,
Earl's mistress clad in soft robe of black sable.

Fireside tales told by a white-haired bard,
sore throat is quick cured with roast boar lard.

Will-o'-the-Wisp's glimmer in marsh gas,
black buboed bodies to plague-pits pass.

Nocturnal vigil of a new knight,
hangman ties hemp halter tight.

Smith forges horseshoe for old grey mare,
three fearless bulldogs bait a brown bear.

A foul-mouthed drunkard sleeps in the stocks,
ploughman wakes to loud crowing of cocks.

A sennet sounds loud on playhouse stage,
cross-gartered stockings are all the rage.

Mendicant friars live with the poor,
bailiff sets traps to snare wrongdoer.

Carp grow plump in the Abbot's fishpond,
ale-wife brews ale, strong brown and blond.

A sheriff hangs those not paying tax,
for high treason nobles face the axe.

Night falls as the curfew tocsin sounds,
the bishop's huntsmen recall their hounds.

Watchman sights ships and lights beacon fires,
gargoyles spout rainwater from church spires.

Queen sits under baldaquin of silk,
wanton Abbess bathes in asses' milk.

A Lord upholds his *droit de seigneur*,
'bride' treats bruises with tincture of myrrh.

Invaders feet set down on wet sand,
an army awaits the King's command.

Monks scribe history on calf vellum page,
for living memory fades as men do age.

Love at a Distance

On our secret beach barefoot, we stand
a pair, but distant from each other,
about a circle, toe-drawn in the sand,
a 'Covid' rite for lass and lover.

Transfixed in mutual blink-free gaze
we skirt the edge of our proscribed ring,
to show the virus will not erase
the evident joy our love does bring.

We each do yearn to catch the other
as we pro-lust are so well-disposed.
But our intimate dreams we smother
at the safe distance by law proposed.

You play a striptease with your white blouse.
"Two hundred years to adore each breast;"
I know how Marvell's verse does you arouse
and how pert the cool breeze makes your chest.

Our circuit's now engulfed by wavelets,
our moist feet grow ankle-socks of sand,
the sun shines off your silver bracelets,
as we part with a chaste wave of hand.

Ancient and Modern

A priest in cassock, surplice and black tippet,
   greets the cortège at the lychgate wicket,
a symbolic threshold twixt this world and the next.
'Man has but a short time to live': the parson's text.

The great, iron-bound, oak mausoleum door
stands open, as it had on countless times before.
Six pall bearers shoulder a purple cloth-draped bier -
an elm coffin atop - their expressions sad and drear.

A cold miasma from the family vault eddies about
black-ribboned mourners, who enter from without
to range round a funeral table crafted from sandstone,
carved with skull, hourglass and crossed thighbone.

The verger lights best beeswax candles in stand and sconce
to cast flickering light about caskets that contained life once.
On brick shelves and stone tiers lie the remains of the dead:
bones, nails, elm planks, shroud shreds, oxidised sheet lead.

A space, next to a dust-crusted coffin with wreath, brittle-dried,
   is labelled with brass plate and ready to be occupied.
He is brought to lie side-by-side with his pre-deceased wife
his partner joined now in death, as once she was in life.

The solemn theatricality of a funeral and committal
fills hearts with grief, makes bereaved memories prickle.
A soul has crossed the bar: life's candle's been snuffed out.
Earth, ashes, dust. Death leaves the living nothing to doubt.

The garden of remembrance is the Council's best,
no pets allowed, no smoking, no food, no singlet vest.
A columbarium stands empty, scattering is the norm.
The trees need water, rabbits have left them chewed, forlorn.

The crematorium's chrome-and-glass sliding door
opens on an infra-red signal from a sensor in the floor.
Friends, family, coats and shopping take up spaces,
a well-known cadaver leaves few available places.

A Tannoy sounds in pre-recorded, genteel, female tones,
"Please behave respectfully and turn off mobile phones."
An assistant wheels in the coffin with one-handed ease,
the weightless shell is pine-veneered to save deciduous trees.

Fresh flowers are ranged behind screen of fine plate glass
so pollen-borne allergens can't to mourners pass.
The fragrant aromas expected from such a floral array
are hypoallergenic scents from a computer-driven spray.

Funeral words are said by a tweed-suited humanist,
reading the deceased's eulogy from a short pro-forma list.
A button is pressed and the coffin slides effortlessly away
to the sound of a Sinatra CD playing *I Did It My Way*.

An employee performs one last service for the deceased
as cremains are released to a chill wind from the Northeast.
Grey ashes swirl from scattering box, lit by a watery sun.
Nothing remains, job sheet's signed, worker's shift is done.

Choosing the Hereafter

A sentry owl atop an old gateway.
Behind, an ancient manor: ivied, grey.
Still rooms echo with empty, silent sound.
A shroud of dust lies even on the ground.
From Purgatory, shades of the recent dead appear;
their mortal shells rest still on catafalque and bier.

The Church cancelled post-mortem judgement,
and Hell's torments seem now less repugnant.
Heaven's peace and eternal tranquillity of mind
have, by modern theologians, been left behind.

Souls are now able to choose their own hereafter
with contemplative thought and sometimes laughter.
'Pick your own forever', is the brochure's phrase,
'a once a lifetime choice, which you can never erase.'

At midnight the marketplace for undecided Souls begins
it's free choice for all with no need to account past sins.
Satan and Gabriel see how many they can each reel in.
Some Spirits need long thought, others a mere coin spin.

Like a madding crowd at an agricultural fair,
the wraiths eddy, tumble and eventually pair
with their chosen angels, who charge no joining fee,
but give gifts of golf clubs or premier cru Chablis.

Hell offers jazz, women, venery, song
and free wine bars open by day and all night long.
Heaven promises 24-hour gyms, theatrical entertainment
and a bespoke, Gucci-designed, exclusive, wingèd raiment.

Hell hopes to ensnare libertines and the morally weak,
Heaven pledges a golf handicap of one, within a week.
Traditions don't die, deals with Satan are signed in blood
as they have always been, since before Old Noah's Flood.

The hourglass runs empty, it is the last chance.
Death, with familiar scythe, leads the Final Dance.
The souls jig and prance over the hills and far away
to Heaven or Hell? No mortal can ever know or say.

These verses are nonsensical, a jaded poet's whimsy,
but from the reverie comes resolution not so flimsy:
we'll enjoy Heaven and Hell now while we live and lust
and cease all anxiety about death until we're coffin dust.

We'll accept the finite: mortality's intrinsic to human life.
There's nothing in the hereafter, so end prodromal strife.
Let your free will guide you to experience living life anew.
The joys of life with no fear of death are such a heady brew.

Stone Testaments

Churchyard laid between old yew trees.
Sepulchral ghosts from ages past
dance where flowers host the honeybees
and where life-fuelled pastimes never last.

Stark and ancient tombstones,
smudged by mossy-lichen green
mark the presence of old bones
as they towards each other lean
to gossip in their neighbour's ear
about lives once lived by those below
where death no longer rules by fear
and eternity's the same tomorrow.

Those quickened ones who come to gaze
and reflect the brevity of a lifelong day
are the unscythed shadows of sunlight's haze
who know night must fall, come what may.

haiku

woodpecker sharp taps
blindman stick scrapes cobblestones
rifles rat-a-tat

nightingale's sweet song
aural stanzas to enthral
even tone-deaf ears

fenland bitterns boom
sound pictures of ancient times
reeds once harvested

dawn chorus birdsong
frogs and toads wear no feathers
but sing at nighttime

on the brink of dawn
crisp linen sheets shine pink-grey
blackbirds greet the day

eyes follow bird flight
curves drawn across evening sky
towards setting sun

moorhens cluck and dart
riverside fowl flotilla
paddles serenely

spring reed beds swishing
purple heron unmoving
old carp lies hidden

startled night-heron
black-and-white feathers flutter
new moonlit silence

flamingos gaggle
flapping rose-red cloud rises
revealing lagoon

guano-white rock
cream-foamed restless waves surround
wedding cake for gulls

cranes fly to the south
straight lines ruled across the sky
lost loves wander free

barn owl's slow wing beats
brief shadows on moonlit reeds
vole scared still with fear

storks pace rice paddy
peacocks perch in camphor tree
gulls scavenge refuse

two robins singing
each claims the territory
twixt fishpond and lawn

skylark's song ascends
tiny heart beats silently
raven's graveyard caw

fresh-ploughed earth furrows
grey-backed herons flying fast
russet leaves falling

Laurel Wreaths

Oppressive high summer heat
Saps energy from woodland sylphs
lounging listlessly in forest glades;
humid, heavy air cloys their breaths.

Shy dryads peep from their oaks,
leaves lie sleepy still in lifeless droops.
Thick moss drapes stream bed stones
muffling sparkling sounds of tinkling rills.

An evening zephyr from Western lands
tousles leafy boughs and stirs fern fronds.
Night sudden falls as distant Pan pipes
stir shaggy satyrs to exercise latent lusts.

Daphne, a water nymph of great beauty,
greets dawn bathing in crystal-clear springs.
The cool waters cascading down her breasts
make her a pert allure no living soul can resist.

A passing beardless, athletic youth is smitten
by Eros' gold-tipped dart, for he desires the naiad's love.
Daphne's alabaster perfection's naïve to the ways of passion
and she runs to escape her perceived ravisher.

But this ephebe is no casual Arcadian passer-by,
he's Zeus's handsome son, the Archer-God, Apollo.
He chases Daphne, who escapes to the riverbank
to invoke the protection of the River-God, her father.

He roots his daughter's dainty feet in riverside loam.
Pale arms he turns to branches clad in leaves of evergreen.
Her blonde hair through speckled sunlight shows
and her beauty in the deep green gloss of foliage shines.

Turned into a laurel tree, Daphne's perfection remains unsullied.
Apollo's love never abates, Daphne's tree he adopted as his own.
He garlands its leaves about the brows of mankind's heroes
to honour them as worthy of being called noble laureates.

A Day at the Seaside by Numbers

Trippers arrived on the nine forty-five, first train of the day,
a 2-6-4 steamer which hissed to a stop on platform three.
Their first stop was the tourist shop and information display,
lunch is twelve thirty till one, but all pamphlets are free.

Six pals had a ten-percent discount for the Pierrot show.
"A number fifty-five 'hop-on-and-off' bus drops you at the door,
99 ices on sale in the foyer," said a tour guide in the know,
"and later, try the beer and whelks in the bar at 'Number Four'.

"In town, there's a twenty-mile-per hour limit in place.
Take care on the hill at the top of the 1887 Jubilee Drive,
the Council's thirty-seater, open-top bus drivers always race.
It's criminal behaviour, the road's a gradient of one-in-five."

The accident, at six fifty-nine by the clock in 'The Grand',
occurred when one of the pals, seven sheets to the wind,
was hit by a number two bus speeding down the strand.
He fell under its front wheels, his legs broken and skinned.

One mate called 999. A helicopter was soon at hand
and took him to hospital: unconscious, deathly-still.
The five gathered in 'Four for Tea' café on the sand,
with heartbeats at twenty to the dozen, all felt a chill.

"Charge to two hundred ... ready," said the medic, "Clear!
...nothing, charge to four hundred ...ready... pray to heaven.
The alcohol's made his heart arrhythmic and unsteady. Clear!
... still nothing. I'm calling it, death timed at twenty forty-seven."

Marriage

A conscious awareness of being alive
enables mortals to live and thrive.
The infinite richness of human existence
is enhanced, with much persistence,
when a man has the heart of a passionate wife
to share and enjoy a well-lived life.
Existentialists employ specious argument to agree
that if one wife is 'good', why not have three?
Such sophistry, to some, may seem sound reason
to regard infidelity as an ever-open season.
A successful marriage is, by Eastern sages, said
to be more than four bare legs and a comfortable bed.
Variety in amorous experiences gives physical pleasures rife,
and a voluptuous mistress adds exotic spice to married life.

I was a sexual gymnast exercising the whole night long
as she adopted Karma Sutra poses with a flexible ease.
I was as Antony in Cleopatra's fabled pompoir clutch
with her between, or kneeling, or lying atop, or on her side,
or underneath, or on all fours, or vigorously astride.

Marriage's mundane intimacies make love's cavorting hard,
but sex need not be predictable and can be avant-garde.

Though she seemed untouchable, as aloof as her sober perm,
she cast off, with wanton smile, pink winceyette from body firm
and, with no respect for the integrity of the blue-rinse crust,
freed her sexual virago of primordial needs and eye-bright lust.
Solomon's Song had been well learned by my most sensual dove.
She was on fire, consumed with desire, passion and mutual love.

Wedded bliss is a creation of constant practice and high art.
A state of mind where couples act in harmony with their heart.
Passion, love and joy will reign supreme — until divorced by death
— if spouses plough their own furrow while they have breath.

Judas

For pecuniary reward Judas would with perfidy comply
And, for thirty pieces of silver, The Messiah he'd identify.
On the agreed night in Gethsemane's Garden he'd pass by,
meet and betray Him with a kiss and call Him rabbi.

Of those gathered beneath the olive trees in that park
were men with chains to bind the man kissed there in the dark.
They feared Him, the King of the Jews, as He could likely spark
the mob to rebel and on the path of revolution to embark.

Silver shekels spilled from the purse of soft goat's leather.
Lightning and rolling thunder showed Yahweh's displeasure.
The affirming bonds of devotion and respect the 'kiss' did sever.
The betrayer, tainted by Satan, would be a pariah forever.

The Court of the Sanhedrin, cosseted in scarlet robes sublime,
enshrined hypocrisy and schemed with plans malign.
The Nazarene's derogation was against laws, temporal and divine,
but the betrayal had suited their political designs just fine.

With barefaced lies and evidence quite unjustified
the man from Nazareth was sentenced to be crucified.
Judas felt a crushing remorse his conscience could not abide
and decided his only possible atonement was suicide.

The silver pieces could no longer be returned
as blood had been spilled by the way they were earned.
Judas' mind with images of perpetual torment burned
as his hemp-haltered body from redbud branch slow turned.

haiku

moisture-laden grass
raindrops from silent tree ferns
sound on old bucket

silent mountain ash
tight-wrapped buds unravelling
fanfare of bright green

old tamarisk tree
grey doves hide in foliage
brush strokes on vellum

catkins on hazel
brave the winter's cold and dark
flowers await spring

silver birch catkins
pollen spread by breeze and bees
sap also rises

tumbling woodland stream
rattling eucalyptus leaves
close your eyes to hear

withered hawthorn hedge
once gave edible spring leaves
close nestled in thorns

music of the breeze
pine tops dance a perfumed waltz
moving clouds aside

goat willow catkins
proud standing pollinators
waiting for breezes

copse of rowan trees
pentangle on leafy floor
naked witches dance

oak-grown mistletoe
golden sickle flashing bright
pagans dance at night

coppiced osiers
willow-wand basket woven
coffin for our love

leafless elm branches
gnarled fringes dressed in snow
life awaits the spring

stone garden stillness
wind-rustled pink cherry trees
nature defines us

tumbling woodland stream
rattling eucalyptus leaves
close your eyes to hear

Et in Arcadia, Ego

Dawn shattered night with shards of yellow fire.
Sparrows chirped greetings as they woke.
A milkmaid trudged half-awake feet towards a low stone byre
to charge the pails made fast to her wooden shoulder-yoke.

Her swain, abed and dreaming of her ample creamy breast,
yawned, arose and donned his cross-stitched linen smock.
The ring of matins bells, carried on a breeze veering to the west,
told Parson Bates it was time to serve his sin-stained flock.

His curate, Dobson Bell, penned sonnets to his heart's ease,
Mary Jones the schoolmistress, of raven hair and sparkling smile.
For her love, as Bell's iambics claimed, he'd die to please,
should she permit him to walk her down the aisle.

Farmer's boys loaded stooks of golden, plump-eared wheat
onto hay wains for Shire horses to pull to old oak barns.
Merry raggle-taggle gipsies gleaned the cornfields bare and neat,
while weavers sat round the duck pond telling ancient yarns.

The Plough's landlord broached a hogshead of best bitter
ready for 'Harvest Home': a feast with dancing till early morn.
Butcher Wilf slaughtered Old Spot suckling pigs by the litter,
his wife Esther busy with black puddings and potted brawn.

The church array of produce mirrored Eden's before the fall,
sweet-singing choirs completed the illusion of Paradise on earth.
Tom, the baker, made meringues, each the size of a Giant Puffball;
of fruit pies and cream-filled pastry cakes there was no dearth.

An itinerate tinker carefully tuned his well-rubbed fiddle,
ready for the cider-fuelled stomping in the festooned parish hall.
A poet's paean, celebrating his experience of living a bucolic idyll,
was declaimed in public to a raucous reception by one and all.

Meanwhile, twelve-year-old Horatio, the cobbler's only son,
died of sweaty fever, his parents prostrated with despair.
For them no celebration of earthly pleasures, joy and fun.
Only stark reality that, even in Arcady, Death is ever there.

Sibilant Sheila

Singer-songwriter, Sheila Simpson soaked splendid summer's solstice sunshine
sunbathing supine besides shrimp-sellers' stalls skirting Scarborough's strand.
Sands surrounding Skegness, Saltburn and Shanklin, sported a similar shoreline,
as so secret stretches in South Shields and select situations in southern Scotland.

Suffering seizures and spastic stomach symptoms since seriate snakebites in 'seventy-six.
Then she'd sensed sweet cicely, celandine, sage smells spreading from shady cypress.
As she sniffed, six secreted spotted serpents, stung sunburned Sheila's spindly sticks
severely, on the soft sensitive skin under her short, skimpy, see-through sundress.

Strange to say, Shelia's subsequent songwriting steamed with sex and seemed superfluously scortatory.
Her seemingly sempiternal, though somewhat superficial saccharine syntax she'd subconsciously suppressed.
Screeds of self-centred scribblings showed Sheila's suicism in several stanzas.
Sheila sobbed senselessly as her sore sensitive psyche suffered severe sadness and suicidal symptoms.
She secretly self-harmed; significant seizures, spasms, stentorian snoring shattered her sleep cycle.
Shedloads of sinister signals, symptomatic of cyclothymic psychosis, surfaced.
Savvy Swiss psych, Sigismund, sedated Sheila; her psychological state subsequently softened.
Seeking salvation from stress, saw spends on psychoanalytical sessions soar sensationally steeply.

Siggy suggested six semesters solitude sequestered in a Sigma-Psi sorority,
where Sheila scoffed superfoods: soused sprats, spiced squid,
and seared seabed scallops with shredded scallions,
all superseded by Scottish smoked salmon soufflé, side-by-side with sardines and sweetbreads of spiced superiority.
For sweetmeats, several servants served sultana shortcakes and sickly-sweet sherry syllabubs.

She sang second soprano in sisterhood sextets, suited similar in six, sensually split, scarlet sarongs.
Seamen's shanties and softly sung 'Shenandoah' suffered her sense of sadness to swell significantly.
Serenades to senoritas, sporting silk shawls, seemed suitably sisterly songs,
as did sung sapphic sonnets celebrating sirens seducing sailors with Circe's spell.

Sheila searched song-sheet shops for scores suitable for singing in shirt sleeves,
scribing, in spidery scrawling script, the saltiest soulful selection onto superfine scraped sheepskin
smattered with a sensational soundscape of staves of syncopated scales of semibreves.
Sheila's especially suggestive sub-edited song was subtitled, 'Seashell on a String'.

Supremely self-centred, also sycophantic, Sheila sent this special self-scored single song
To stupendously stunning sensual superstar songstress, Sandie, sans-shoes (sic), Shaw.
Sheila sought a soulmate's support. Sandie stayed stony silent, steadfastly shtum.
So solitary Sheila started solo, selling seashells on the seashore.

1960: Dog Latin for Beginners

A naïve undergrad, not yet nineteen,
lusted for the daughter of his college Dean.
This *puella pulchra*, beautiful girl,
did cause his hormones to dance and whirl.
Sed audaces Fortuna juvat,
Fortune favours the bold, he knew that
and yearned that his arms would soon enfold
such a pulchritudinous centrefold.

They met, by chance, in the sandstone quad,
he desired her consensual nod.
"*Te amo,* love does conquer all;
in time you'll have me firmly in thrall.
Now it's *in promptu* sex I'm wanting
- please do excuse my fervid panting.
Let's have coitus, lewd coupling, right soon
and live *dulcis vita*, a sweet life, in my bedroom.

"*Nos cedamus amori*, I've often said,
we must yield to ardour when abed.
The time's ripe for me to lose my cherry,
so *gaudeamus*, let's both be merry
and mutually enjoy the fun of carnal play.
Carpe diem, seize - just for the two of us - the day,
we are the bright young ones, *juvenes sumus*,
eager for sex now, before we're graveyard humus."

"Lover," she said, "cease these honeyed words,
let's screw now and chatter-on afterwards.
I'm not nunnery-taught, in fact *non virgo intacta*
and, as you'll soon find out, I'm a fervent enactor.
On a car's back seat, in the open air and in bed
duco non ducor, I lead but am not led.
I love, *sic parvus magna*, just so as you know,
playing with small things and watching them grow."

Itium atque itium, like pulsing beat of drum
again and again, till they both felt numb.
Though much vigorous sex was as intended
fatigue set in and *tantum strenuus sexus* ended.
They're as happy as *vaccae*, cows, in fields of clovers
and they each pledge fidelity as future lovers.
They float on *nubes novem*, a cloud-nine daze,
Imagining never ending sex for *septimana*, seven days.

It happened that, while doing his rounds,
the dean overheard soft humping sounds
and his daughter's high soprano cry,
"*dulce mori*, sweet death, I'm to die."
He found her mouthing a fervent Benedictus,
her flushed face set in beatific, yet venal, rictus.
He was speechless, the bed seemed a metaphor
for his daughter's lust-filled downfall if not more.

"I've found *verus amor*, the true love of my life,"
said the student, "I've no more existential strife."
"*Finis*," said the Dean, "your imagination's running rife,
she's my darling daughter, not your married wife.
This is *aegri somnia*, a nightmare of a dream,
I see her grin, *cattus habet crepito*, a cat that's got cream.
Just like mother, loose and randy with any Dick or Andy.
Ego sum defessus, I'm worn out and need a brandy.

"Your bedmate's my daughter and I'm your dean.
Your brain's turned off, there's a problem unforeseen.
By law, my relationship with you is *in loco parentis*,
you are almost my adopted son, a moral apprentice.
I must provide guidance as substitute mum and dad
until you are twenty-one and your majority be had.
I can't allow you to have sex while in my care
or I'll break the law and be sued: that's not fair.

"Future's grim, you were caught *in flagrante delicto*
by me, the Dean, with my dear daughter, having a go.
You've done things of a type both lurid and sexual.
I believe you when you claim it was wholly consensual
mutual lovemaking: *vice versa* and *quid pro quo*.
But it's clear, from this *alma mater* you will have to go.
The penalty for brazen undergraduate fornication
is, *sine exceptio*, an immediate rustication."

Nature conspired to frustrate this proposal
as all mankind creates life at Fate's disposal.
The Dean acted timely with wisdom and decorum,
though he felt somewhat jaded, *non felix leporem*,
he'd lost his joy for life and was not a happy bunny,
just a worried father, no pains ominous or funny.
His daughter was pregnant, unmarried and he was stressed,
though he was proud with a grandchild to be blessed.

The student, the Dean's grandchild's *pater*,
sought to complete his studies at his *alma mater*.
The academic court reversed his suspension.
The Dean, keen to ensure no misapprehension,
warned the student, "No more *dolce usque niente*,
living the life of Riley with pleasures a plenty,
unless it's with my daughter, *id est* your new wife,
or *et castratus eris,* gelded by my rusty knife."

Diogenes, the Cynic, Views Love's Seasonal Changes From his Barrel

His love's heart, devoid of pulsing beat,
had no more need of summer heat.
Autumnal chills she'd now avoid,
her soul had tumbled down death's lonely void.

His endless tears of unrequited grief
dropped wet on winter-holly leaf.
But now his eyes do dance in springtime's light
as his latest true love hoves into sight.

Autumn Sonnet: 12.x.2023

I move dreamlike amongst the part-used men,
with breath that barely mists a mirror's face
and tortoise gait that can't compete or race.
Of dates, places, times I've but a vague ken
my memory fails me every now and then.
There are friends' monikers I just can't place,
nor can I name that familiar face.
Writing's hard, thoughts no longer flow to pen.
Flashbacks from golden days of years ago,
remind how plaudits did echo and swarm,
when I was laureate of life's great maze.
Now, my mind has no eager throb and glow,
black dog my spirit does downward transform
old conceits echo in my autumn days.

haiku

wood-ash blown by breeze
settles on chrysanthemums
grey shroud for past love

mountain hyacinth
clusters of blue grape flowers
wine only for bees

yellow-blossomed broom
vanilla scents on sea breeze
summer holidays

spring-burst daffodils
chrome yellow swathes on green grass
white daisy necklace

sun opens rose buds
deep crimson perfumed flowers
brown decay follows

sedge-thatched cottages
tall hollyhocks rose arbours
empty chocolate box

grey-green sea thistle
sharp-set leaves against the wind
salt tang memories

deceitful daisy
white open face greets the day
closed pink-tipped at dusk

daffodils on grass
a body-sized mass of turf
graves will come to pass

silent snowdrops shoot
white green-leafed stars on brown ground
nodding in spring breeze

buttercups nettles
skeleton-bikes and sofas
fly-tipped abstract art

Recipe for Pain

Take a couple of lovers,
fresh or leftovers.

Spice with jealousy's green eye,
or juice of whopping great lie.

Add a ripe letter from an old flame,
addressed to him or her, it's all the same.

Let them stew separately and alone,
without email or mobile phone.

Suspicion's natural yeast will ferment
a toxic brew of thoughts of malintent.

Scatter seeds of distrust, enough to sow strife
dust with steamy images of the other's secret life.

Leave ingredients to bake wrapped in anguish overnight.
Serve heartache's insufferable pain, fresh by morning light.

Playing My Part

The curtain rises, I stand centre stage,
a newfound amateur winging my part.
Self-knowledge affords me a flying start
as lead actor in my own life and age.
I play child, youth, adult, decrepit sage.
I'm taught essential things to make me smart
but fail to understand an aching heart,
or how the pain of loving to assuage.
I sense wonder, passion, excitement, joy
as books lead me through imagination's realm.
Bittersweet Love and Loss form emotions
but these can never be allowed to cloy
for fear feelings might logic overwhelm
and leave my mind drifting whimsy's oceans.

haiku

blue-grey woodsmoke wisps
curl sharp pinpricks in my eyes
memories make tears

soft windless raindrops
moisture beads on upturned face
hide salt tears of loss

regular sleeping
a nocturnal preamble
to a random death

sulphur scent hot springs
steam water droplets on face
tears in poet's eyes

skaters' blades cut deep
etched message on ice parchment
read in near silence

stone marker tells all
date of first and final breath
but not that feet smell

good fairies dancing
toadstool rings at midnight hour
childhood images

rare bronze urn patina
dull reflection of your life
graceful sheen of death

weather changes skies
recreating humdrum lives
and our very selves

sweet incense smoke curls
skywards touching the white clouds
pleasing to my gods

restlessness of mind
stormy violence of the seas
silence of snowflakes

collages are sharp-snipped
images from what once was
foremost in my mind

monosyllables
life love joy loss pain hate know
small words giant thoughts

distant temple gong
another soul passes on
mist shrouds graveyard stones

grey winter dawn light
empty dust-covered choir stalls
wooden coffin-rests

shrine of old sea gods
native girl brings fresh-picked fruits
Xmas on Bali

gong echoes loud
prayer wheels tinkle in cool breeze
Lama prays alone

it's Shirley surely
poster girl for ringlets curls
and hooch-free cocktails

A Short History of Pippins

Adam, a sensible Yorkshire lad, pocketed a packet of pippin pips,
before being evicted from Eden by sword with flaming tips.
He planted the pips on his return home to live in God's own land
and English pippin trees thrived under his green-fingered hand.

Adam's pippins are ubiquitous, they've spread to every land,
except those frozen polar wastes and hot deserts full of sand.
Apples are ever-popular fruit with a place in old folklore.
As symbols for 'eureka moments' they really are quite core.

Doubtless one of Adam's ripe pippins fell on Newton's head,
sans Isaac's Laws of Gravity, we'd still by old wives' tales be led.
We learned an apple for the teacher helped pupils evade the cane
and a daily dose kept doctors at bay, the living free from pain.

At the first Miss World, Love won the golden pippin prize,
Goddesses' hissy fits and war with Troy did then materialise.
Death by apple for female beauties is more than rumoured hunch,
a wicked witch gave Snow White a poisoned pippin for her lunch.

It was a pippin William Tell impaled atop his young son's head,
to prove an independent Switzerland was viable, not dead.
There was never a Swiss Renaissance with new ideas that shock.
The Cantons' only legacy: milk chocolate and the cuckoo clock.

Adam's pippins found their way to the United States of A;
there, Johnny Appleseed sowed pips each and every day.
Racehorses receive an apple when their race is won.
A Big Apple logo marked New York City as *the* place for fun.

It is strange that Adam's apples are not found on any tree,
nor are apple-pie beds displayed in a patisserie.
The apple of our eye is not to one's optical system hard-wired.
Though Nell Gwynn sold oranges, it was her apples men desired.

This history of pippins brings Yorkshire folk good tidings.
Finest baked apple pies are from mothers in't Three Ridings.

False Memories

Memory is like a slippery eel
especially when it comes to how you feel.
Were there thoughts of affection in your head,
or purely lust that steered her to bed?

Your memories flowed false when he was dead,
his reputation by excess was fed
your image of him, uniformed and proud
was smoke and mirrors, just a cloud.

Recollection was her voice by angels was endowed,
and on stage by fans, she was applauded loud.
Truth be told she sang sharply shrill and off-key
and her phrasing was decidedly at sea.

I remember our surfing a tunnel off Waikiki.
Those great waves brought us close, just you and me,
Like in a 'Beach Boys' movie with free-living broads.
But, let's be honest, I've never ridden a surfboard.
All my life I've lived in Leeds,
… never been close to the sea,
… never even been abroad.

A Reminder

I stand, as a reminder of *our* past
in the last pew on the left.
You leave the vestry in ecstasy,
welded to *his* arm,
until my face you spy.
Your beaming countenance falters
like a cat that's got sour cream.

The Truth About Eve

Imagine an antique etching of an old apple tree
and, as sure as sponge is served with afternoon tea,
your mind to Eve and her proffered apple will be drawn
and thoughts of Eden's scheming serpent will soon spawn.

Folk are aghast at the true history of Eve and the apple,
when they hear the lies with which they now must grapple.
In the beginning, that primordial gardener, God Almighty,
filled his allotment with fruit trees, ferns and cacti spiky.

In a corner, an apple tree was home to a truly streetwise snake,
a board-certified philosopher who knew all things true and fake.
God placed the fruit of that tree out of bounds to Adam and Eve
to prevent the serpent gifting them the insight to perceive.

Eve's inquisitive mien caused God's proscription to be breached
and she took to heart immediately what the snake had teached.
Poison ivy, not shame, caused Eve to be of her nakedness aware
and hide her sensitive bits, though Adam still did drool and stare.

Mankind now had awareness, thanks to an Aristotelian adder.
This wasn't God's intention, which made Him all the madder.
To rectify the PR failure, He reached out to Professor Freud,
an expert in erogenous zones and the primaeval haemorrhoid.

It was false news to suggest the serpent led Eve into original sin
with a suggestive phallic wiggle and its tongue's convincing spin.
Adam's earthy lusts gave Eve power to tantalise and enthral,
but man wasn't led by lusting loins alone to his own downfall.

The Almighty, a creative force *sans pareil,* loved playing God.
Some immortal works were of the best, others were just cod.
That Eve suffered moral turpitude from viperish temptation
was God's deceit: Eve's tutorial was the start of Man's salvation.

Kant finds truth when thought is congruent with the real thing,
not when you sink your laughing gear into a Bramley's seedling.
Eve did well when she heeded the sophisticated asp's descant
and let Humanism into our lives to counterbalance biblical cant.

Ovid's Great Mistake

In 8 BCE, the Roman poet Publius Ovidius Nasso was, for reasons still unknown, exiled from Rome by decree of Caesar Augustus. Ovid, author of, inter alia, **Ars Amatoria** *(The Art of Love), died in exile near Constantia on the Black Sea in 17 CE. In 2017 the Council of the City of Rome revoked Ovid's banishment, 2,000 years after it began.*

In the *Ars Amatoria* ...

you advised maids seeking lovers to enhance their charms
by removing the hairy goats which lurked beneath their arms.
On this count, dear Ovid, you are wrong: believe you me.
Was this advice the reason you were exiled to the Black Sea?

Deep in our rustic memory grottoes, animal urges lurk,
awaiting a suitable trigger to render us wantonly berserk.
Priapus rules all in this garden of earthy animal lust,
which lies on the dark side of a lover's implicit trust.

Let Pan and his cloven-hoofed brothers play the ancient pipes,
wild passion is not found indulging missionary archetypes.
Inhale instead the musky aroma of your mistresses' armpits,
and release your dormant satyr with a primaeval spritz.

The Somme - With Addendum 11.xi.2023

The Somme basin, the centre stage of that cataclysmic first Great War,
was where Prehistoric Man had fished and hunted down wild boar.
For aeons man had joined Nature with due respect and all humility
to harvest the rolling lands the ancient Celts named for their tranquillity.

All placidity vanished when the grey-and-khaki uniformed hordes came
to rape the ground with earthworks ready for the start of that 'Big Game'.
The hills echoed to marching boots, which churned roads into an oozing fen
as did hooves of horses, soldiers' constant pals since times of Trojan men.

Birdsong vanished from the land as if Mother Earth had tolled a bell
and declared from then on there'd be silence in this man-made Hell,
save for the rare time when a lonely skylark ascended singing to the skies
and bloodied men on hearing it paused their butchery to pipe their eyes.

Battles are archived by winner's name and the number of the dead.
It matters not, in great schemes of War, how individual lives are shed.
Such knowledge would cut families right to their souls' collective core
if they saw their menfolk's mangled bodies in fly-blown shrouds of gore.

The pain of bayonet stabbing flesh and eviscerating belly sac
is different from that of deep leg wound turning a gangrenous black,
or when, with smell of musty hay, phosgene shreds lungs and asphyxiates,
or in collapsed trench, the lonely soldier is buried alive and suffocates.

The battlefields act as everlasting memorials for the dead.
Erstwhile soldiers sleep forever snug inside their marble bed.
The quick, without hesitation, remember the soldier dead and eulogise.
However, the group sacrifice, pro patria, does individuals depersonalise.

Pain suffered by a soldier killed in the War was unique to them,
an individual agony, no memorial could represent nor another ken.
Death by bayonet, gas, shrapnel, shell, bullet, gangrene and more
prowled ever-ready with the rats about the trench's mud-deep floor.

Lessons lie unheeded, though a hundred years have passed.
'They' vowed and pledged 'that War' would surely be the last.
Current existential wars demand fresh bodies on pyres be piled.
Battlefields are urban. The dead civilian: the old, a woman, a child.

It is now an ironic aphorism, "dulce et decorum est pro patria mori"
when the massacre of the defenceless is the cost of glory.
War is depraved, lacks sanity, gnaws at Civilisation's precious moral core.
It must cease, lest it force mankind into a dystopian hell for evermore.

If

If you'd rather sip a Côte d'Or Montrachet
than glug a generic boxed wine dubbed 'vin Blanc'
If you favour Gevrey Chambertin with a Grand Cru cachet
and refuse to drink retsina or red commercial plonk.

If you have turbot poached because taste does matter
and eat Beluga caviar fresh from the Caspian Sea.
If you've never had a Mars bar deep-fried in batter,
nor offered guests an ice-cold can of sweetened tea.

If your breakfast cuppa is always first-flush Darjeeling
and served with lemon, as milk is taste-congealing.
If you take black puddings with cubes of best pork fat
and never let 'Yorkshire Puds' turn out dismal flat.

If you eat your steak 'tartare' and never in a bun
and drink with it a champagne brut, 'blanc de noirs'.
If snipe on toast for luncheon is your dream of Elysium,
and favourite dinner's at Raymond Blanc's 'Le Manoir'.

If you can't imagine a thick slice of boiled York Ham
... without salivating,
then you are a Yorkshireman!

Yorkshire Day, 1. viii.2022

Carpe Diem

Now Time drags by slowly in the afternoon
as I watch the falling hourglass sands alone.
Once 'now' was commitment far too soon,
I'd do 'it' tomorrow, Time seemed mine to own.

By candlelight I journeyed far and wide in dusty pages,
gleaning knowledge by reading countless reams
of arcane opinions and the wisdom of ancient sages,
'Seize the day', all did say, 'Cease your idle dreams'.

I indulged in restaurants where fine wine did swirl,
such lonely time-wasting did melancholy endorse
and cause that dark child of night his banner to unfurl
to shield me from Eros and his 'life-giving' force.

Daydreams brought harbingers of death's grim reign,
and tedium replaced variety and effort in my daily grind
as, with dimming senses, I wrestled the Fates' skein.
I'm seduced by inertia and quiescence of mind.

I so often failed to seize Fortune's proffered lock,
preferring to laze Time away in idle frivolity.
I wasted Time, broke my life's own clock,
and cold, empty Time doth now waste me.

Ian Hindmarch is a bibliomaniac and collector of all things curious. Reading and dabbling in antiquarian literature and old books on obscure topics have been his favorite pastime since schooldays. Since retiring as Professor Emeritus after forty years of scientific medical research, he started writing short stories and verses. These scribblings were in marked contrast, both in content and style, to the numerous books and papers he wrote and published during his academic career.

Many aspects of the human condition can be found in this current collection, including love, heartache, passion, loss, joy, sex and death. Fables, both biblical and profane, are reimagined and retold. The poems come in several forms: tanka, haiku, villanelle, blank verse, rhyming couplets, pantoum, sonnet. Some are cynical, some nostalgic, or idyllic, or impassioned; others bawdy, or irreverent, or melancholic, or teeming with innuendo, or simply outrageous. A vein of humour or verbal tomfoolery weaves its way through several verses. Nothing is certain.

Ian Hindmarch has his roots in Yorkshire, but he now lives on Kent's East Coast with two Belgians, his wife Niekol and Teddy, a Bouvier des Flandres.